Table of Contents

Introduction

The ketogenic diet is the most popular weight loss regimen to date. It encourages dieters to reduce their carbohydrate intake and increase their fat and protein consumption to push the body to undergo the state of ketosis to burn fat more efficiently. As a result, you lose weight effectively, as well as stabilize your body's physiological statistics, such as your blood pressure, glucose, and cholesterol levels.

While this diet program is really easy to follow, many people still find it difficult to sustain this regimen. One of the biggest reasons why people find it hard to sustain this lifestyle is the complexity of preparing ketogenic-friendly meals.

The thing is, since most ketogenic-friendly meals contain mostly meat, a certain amount of time and dedication is needed to prepare meals. But what if I tell you that you don't need to make complicated recipes to follow the ketogenic lifestyle? As long as you have an air fryer, you will be able to prepare simple, straightforward, and delicious meals that can also help you accelerate your body's fat-burning mechanism.

Moreover, preparing meals with an air fryer is also fun and convenient. It frees up your hands because there's no stirring involved. All there is to it is to pop your dishes inside, turn on the dial and you are good to go.

To learn more about ketogenic air fryer cooking, let this book serve as your ultimate guide to creating ketogenic-friendly meals with your air fryers. Go and read on. Happy reading!

The Ketogenic Diet

Under the ketogenic diet, the body is pushed to the state of ketosis wherein it uses up fat bodies called ketones as its main source of energy instead of glucose. Unlike other short-lived fad diets, the ketogenic diet has been around for more than ninety years as it was first used to treat patients who suffered from epilepsy. Today, it is still used to minimize the effects of epileptic seizures, but it is also used for weight loss.

Understanding the Ketogenic Diet

People who follow the ketogenic diet limit the intake of carbohydrates to around 20 to 30 net grams daily or 5% of the daily diet. Net grams refer to the number of carbohydrates that remain after subtracting the grams of dietary fiber. Since the carbohydrate intake is limited, dieters are encouraged to consume more fat and protein in amounts of 80% and 20%; respectively.

The ketogenic diet is often referred to as a low-carb diet, but it is important to take note that it [ketogenic diet] is entirely different from the other low-carb diets that encourage protein loading. Protein is not as important as fat is in the ketogenic diet. The reason is that the presence of a higher amount of protein pushes the body to the process called gluconeogenesis wherein protein is converted into glucose. If this happens, the body is not pushed to a state of ketosis. This is the reason why it is so crucial to consume more fat under the ketogenic diet than protein.

How Does It Work?

When we eat, the carbohydrates found in the food that we consume is converted into a simple sugar called glucose. Alongside converting carbs to glucose, the pancreas also manufactures insulin, which is a hormone responsible for pushing glucose into the cells to be used up as energy.

As glucose is used up as the main source of energy, the fats that you also consume from food is not utilized thus they are immediately stored in the liver and adipocytes (specialized fat cells). Moreover, if you consume too many carbohydrates, the glucose that is not used up is converted into glycogen and is stored in the liver and muscles as standby energy source. If not used up, it is processed and converted to fat and stored all over the body, thus you gain weight.

However, the body is working in a brilliant system that allows us to use up and burn off fats from our body. The ability of the body to produce ketones is part of the millions of years of the human evolution. It protected our ancestors during times of starvation in the past. During periods of famines in the past wherein the body cannot consume carbohydrates over long periods of time, the body uses up fats as a source of energy, as it does in ketosis. This process has helped our ancestors survived for millions of years. Amazing, right?

So, when does ketosis happen? People usually enter the state of ketosis after 3 to 4 days consuming little amounts of carbohydrates. But to undergo the state of ketosis, some people think that you have to stop eating altogether—but not with the ketogenic diet. The ketogenic diet bypasses starvation by encouraging you to eat more fats and adequate amounts of protein so that you don't have to undergo starvation. So what food should you eat? This particular diet regimen encourages people to consume more fats sourced from healthy and whole food ingredients. That way, the body is pushed to a pure state of ketosis without ever feeling hungry.

Benefits of The Ketogenic Diet

Aside from being used to minimize the effects of seizures among patients who suffer from epilepsy, the ketogenic diet also comes with a lot of benefits. So, if you are not yet convinced to take on this diet regimen, below is a list of the benefits of this particular diet program.

- **Weight loss:** The body will burn stored fats that add most of the bulk to your weight. Eating more fats and proteins also fills your stomach for a long time thus removing any cravings to eat sweet foods and limiting any overeating.

- **Reduce the risk for type 2 diabetes:** Insulin resistance is a common occurrence among people who suffer from Type 2 diabetes. This means that while your body is producing insulin, the hormone is not working properly in pushing the glucose into the cells. As a result, the glucose remains in the bloodstream and wrecks havoc on the other organs of the body. But with the ketogenic diet, the hormone insulin is stabilized, and the blood sugar level is not elevated because you are consuming less carbs.

- **Reduce the risk for heart diseases:** People who are at risk for heart disease can benefit from the ketogenic diet. Studies have shown that heart disease markers, such as triglycerides and cholesterol, go down when following this particular diet.

- **Can help protect against cancer:** Refined sugar is a highly inflammatory food, but since the ketogenic diet limits the consumption of carbs, you'll be able to easily avoid refined and processed sugars. Moreover, the foods that are allowed to eat under this diet regimen all have anti-inflammatory properties and are rich in antioxidants that can fight off cancer cells within the body.

- **Maintains brain function:** Aside from epilepsy, the ketogenic diet can also benefit people who are at risk of developing brain diseases such as dementia, specifically Alzheimer's disease. While the brain requires glucose as its main source of energy, using ketones can alter the cellular energy pathways of the brain, thus improving the brain function. Moreover, this particular diet can also improve your mental awareness, thereby making your more focused and alert.

- **Increased lifespan:** Several studies suggest that people who follow the ketogenic diet are able to live longer than those who consume high amounts of carbohydrates.

- **Better skin quality:** People who suffer from acne breakouts can definitely benefit from eating ketogenic-friendly foods. Many have found that they end up having clearer and better skin quality.

- **Better nutrition:** Foods allowed on this diet offer important antioxidants, vitamins and minerals for your health. Choose non-processed, whole foods for the maximum benefits.

What to Eat and Not to Eat Under This Diet?

This particular diet regimen encourages you to consume healthy fats. Thus, eat fats such as olive oil, avocado, nuts, and seeds. For your protein, eat poultry, fish, beef, pork, and other game meats. Since carbohydrates are limited to only a few net grams, choose leafy vegetables and berries, as they are low in carbohydrate content yet high in vitamins, minerals, and antioxidants.

While the types of foods that you can eat are straightforward, trying to determine the foods that you should limit can be quite challenging. Thus, below is a list of foods that you should limit while following the ketogenic diet.

- **Starchy foods:** Foods rich in starch should be avoided. These include potatoes, pasta, and bread.

- **Confectionaries:** Processed sweet foods made with refined sugar should be avoided on this diet regimen. These may include candies, ice creams, sweet beverages, cakes, and cookies to name a few. Even fresh fruit juice is should be limited because it contains high amounts of fructose.

- **Root vegetables:** Root vegetables are naturally starchy, so limit sweet potatoes, yams, taros, carrots, parsnips, celeriac, and rutabaga to name a few.

- **Most fruits:** Most fruits contain high amounts of fructose and this can elevate the blood sugar level. However, this does not mean that you should avoid fruits altogether. The ketogenic diet still allows fruits such as strawberries, raspberries, and cherries, as they have a high antioxidant content.

- **Beans:** Beans are good sources of protein but also carbohydrates so limit.

- **Low carb products:** Anything that says "low-carb" is marketed healthy but did you know that they can still contain high amounts of sugar?

- **Alcohol:** Alcohol contains high amounts of carbohydrates so be sure to limit it when following this diet.

Understand the Air Fryer

The air fryer is a nifty kitchen appliance that allows you to fry food at high temperature using circulating hot air around the oil. This allows you to cook food evenly and faster compared to baking them in the oven. With this kitchen appliance, food is cooked with a delicious crispy layer, so you get the same effects of fried food without that greasy feel.

How Does It Work?

Air fryers are not only limited to frying food, but it also allows you to cook a wide assortment of food. Air fryers often come with the Rapid Air Technology that circulates extremely hot air of up to 400^0F to cook food.

The air fryer comes with an exhaust fan that is located just above the cooking chamber. This provides an excellent airflow that is required to cook food, even those that are located at the bottom of the basket. The strong fan allows the food to get the same amount of temperature within the chamber. Moreover, it also comes with a cooling system to control the internal temperature so that the food does not burn while in the middle of cooking.

To cook food, place the food in the fryer basket and place the basket in the fryer and you can start cooking. Halfway through, give the basket a good shake in order to distribute the food evenly. The air fryer basket makes it easy to take the food out all at once, without the need to probe through the hot basket. It is as easy as that.

How to Use the Air Fryer

Using the air fryer is no rocket science—you can cook food easily even if you are a kitchen novice. It is important to take note that the air fryer comes with a cooking basket where you can place food. This makes it easier to handle your food while cooking.

First things first, make sure that you plug in the air fryer and allow it to preheat for 4 minutes. Make sure that the chamber is hot enough before putting the food so that the cooking process starts easily.

It is always important to spray cooking oil to the fryer basket in order to avoid food from sticking to the basket. This will also make it easier for you to shake the food in the middle of your cooking time for even frying.

When placing the food in the fryer basket, make sure that you put space between each food so that the hot air can pass through and cook food evenly on all sides. You can use an aluminum foil to separate large chunks of meat, for example, for even cooking.

When marinating the ingredients, make sure that you use dry spice rub as oil and sauces can cause smoke, as well as make cleaning of the air fryer more difficult. Should you need to put sauce or oil, do it at the end of cooking when you have taken out the food from the fryer. Never use high temperature when cooking with fatty foods to avoid messes.

Cleaning the Air Fryer

Cleaning the air fryer is easy and it does not require you to do a lot of complicated tasks. The first thing that you need to do is to unplug the air fryer to prevent electrocution. The basket is dishwasher-friendly, so you can take it out from the fryer's chamber and clean it in the sink or in the dishwasher.

Once you remove the fryer basket, give extra attention to the base of the fryer where most of the drippings from the food have collected and dried. Make sure that you remove the browning that has accumulated at the base as this can lead to burning in future cooking. You can remove the browning by spraying it with warm soapy water and allowing it to soak for at least an hour. This will soften the browning, so you can easily wipe it clean.

Aside from taking care of the inside of the air fryer, it is also important to clean the exterior using a warm moist cloth.

Frequently Asked Questions

It is easy to use the air fryer but if you are a first-time user, you must have a lot of questions about using the air fryer. Below are the frequently asked questions on how to use the air fryer.

1 – Can I cook different foods in the air fryer aside from fried foods?
The air fryer is not limited to cooking only fried foods. You can use it to cook different types of foods like casseroles and even desserts.

2 – How much food do I need to put inside?
Different air fryers tend to have different capacities. If you are not sure how much you need to put in, look for the "max" mark and use it as a guide to fill the basket only to that part.

3 – Can I put in more ingredients while the food is being cooked?
Yes. Just open the air fryer so that you can add the ingredients that you want to put in. There is also no need to change the internal temperature as it can stabilize once you close the air fryer chamber.

4 – Can I put aluminum or baking paper at the bottom of the air fryer?
Yes. You can use both to line the base of the air fryer. However, make sure that you poke holes so that the hot air can pass through the material and cook food thoroughly.

5 – Do I really need to preheat my air fryer?

Preheating the air fryer can reduce the cooking time so you can save energy. Moreover, food comes out crispier. However, if you forgot to preheat, then that is still okay. You can still cook your food, but the quality is not as great as when you preheat the fryer. To preheat the air fryer, simply turn it to the temperature that is needed for cooking and set the timer for 5 minutes. Once the timer turns off, place your food in the basket and continue cooking.

Breakfast Recipes

Air Fryer Frittata

Serves: 1, Preparation Time: 5 minutes, Cooking Time: 10 minutes

Ingredients
- 2 large eggs, beaten
- 1 tablespoon heart-healthy oil
- 1 tablespoon green onions, chopped
- 1 tablespoon chopped red bell pepper
- 1 tablespoon ghee or melted butter
- Salt and pepper to taste

Instructions
1. Preheat the air fryer at 350^0F for 5 minutes.
2. Combine all ingredients in a mixing bowl.
3. Pour the egg mixture into a greased cake pan that will fit in the air fryer.
4. Place the cake pan with the egg mixture in the air fryer.
5. Air fry at 350^0F for 10 minutes.
6. Serve and enjoy!

Nutrition information:
Calories per serving: 374; Carbohydrates: 2 g; Protein: 13 g; Fat: 35 g; Sugar: 1 g; Sodium: 235 mg; Fiber: 0.3 g

Breakfast Scotch Eggs

Serves: 7, Preparation Time: 2 hours, Cooking Time: 25 minutes

Ingredients

- 2 large eggs, beaten
- 1-pound ground beef (85% lean/15% fat)
- 2 tablespoons butter, melted
- ¼ cup coconut flour
- Salt and pepper to taste
- 7 large eggs, boiled and peeled
- Cooking spray

Instructions

1. Preheat the air fryer at 350^0F for 5 minutes.
2. Place the beaten eggs, ground beef, butter, and coconut flour in a mixing bowl. Season with salt and pepper to taste.
3. Coat the boiled eggs with the meat mixture and place in the fridge to set for 2 hours.
4. Grease the air fryer basket with cooking spray and place all the ingredients in it.
5. Place in the air fryer basket, cook at 350^0F for 25 minutes.
6. Serve and enjoy!

Nutrition information:

Calories per serving: 320; Carbohydrates: 1.3 g; Protein: 25.9 g; Fat: 22.9 g; Sugar: 0.5 g; Sodium: 178 mg; Fiber: 0.6 g

Breakfast Radish Hash Browns

Serves: 6, Preparation Time: 5 minutes, Cooking Time: 10 minutes

Ingredients
- 1-pound radish, peeled and grated
- 1 medium onion, chopped
- 1 teaspoon garlic powder
- 1 teaspoon onion powder
- ¾ teaspoon salt
- ½ teaspoon paprika
- ¼ teaspoon ground black pepper
- 3 tablespoon heart-healthy oil
- Cooking spray

Instructions
1. Preheat the air fryer at 350^{0}F for 5 minutes.
2. Place all ingredients in a mixing bowl.
3. Form patties using your hands.
4. Grease with cooking spray before placing individual patties in the air fryer basket.
5. Cook for 10 minutes at 350^{0}F until crispy.
6. Serve and enjoy!

Nutrition information:
Calories per serving: 84; Carbohydrates: 5 g; Protein: 0.9 g; Fat: 6.8 g; Sugar: 2.2 g; Sodium: 322 mg; Fiber: 1.6 g

Air Fried Scrambled Eggs

Serves: 2, Preparation Time: 5 minutes, Cooking Time: 10 minutes

Ingredients
- 2 large eggs, beaten
- 2 tablespoons unsalted butter, melted
- Salt and pepper to taste
- Cooking spray

Instructions
1. Preheat the air fryer at 250^{0}F for 5 minutes.
2. Mix all ingredients in a mixing bowl until well combined.
3. Place in a greased pan that will fit in the air fryer.
4. Cook for 10 minutes at 250^{0}F.
5. Open the air fryer every 2 minutes and fluff with a fork.
6. Serve warm and enjoy!

Nutrition information:
Calories per serving: 174; Carbohydrates: 0.4 g; Protein: 6.5 g; Fat: 16.5 g; Sugar: 0.2 g; Sodium: 73 mg; Fiber: 0 g

Air Fryer Baked Eggs

Serves: 1, Preparation Time: 3 minutes, Cooking Time: 5 minutes

Ingredients
- 1 large egg, whole
- Cooking spray

Instructions
1. Preheat the air fryer at 350^{0}F for 5 minutes.
2. Grease a ramekin with cooking spray and crack the egg gently inside.
3. Place the ramekin in the air fryer basket.

4. Cook for 5 minutes at 350⁰F.

Nutrition information:
Calories per serving: 72; Carbohydrates: 0.4 g; Protein: 6.3 g; Fat: 4.8 g; Sugar: 0.2 g; Sodium: 71 mg; Fiber: 0 g

Air Fryer Egg Cups

Serves: 4, Preparation Time: 5 minutes, Cooking Time: 10 minutes

Ingredients
- 4 large eggs, beaten
- 2 tablespoons butter
- ¼ cup spinach, chopped finely
- Salt and pepper to taste
- 1 bacon strip, fried and crumbled
- Cooking spray

Instructions
1. Preheat the air fryer at 350⁰F for 5 minutes.
2. In a mixing bowl, combine the eggs, butter, and spinach. Season with salt and pepper to taste.
3. Grease a ramekin with cooking spray and pour the egg mixture inside.
4. Sprinkle with bacon bits.
5. Place the ramekin in the air fryer.
6. Cook for 10 minutes at 350⁰F.
7. Serve and enjoy!

Nutrition information:
Calories per serving: 139; Carbohydrates: 0.85 g; Protein: 7.8 g; Fat: 11.5 g; Sugar: 0.3 g; Sodium: 173 mg; Fiber: 0.3 g

Air Fryer Hard Boiled Egg

Serves: 6, Preparation Time: 2 minutes, Cooking Time: 15 minutes

Ingredients
- 6 large eggs

Instructions
1. Preheat the air fryer at 360^{0}F for 5 minutes.
2. Place the eggs in the air fryer basket.
3. Cook for 15 minutes at 360^{0}F.
4. Remove from the air fryer basket and place in cold water.
5. Serve and enjoy!

Nutrition information:
Calories per serving: 72; Carbohydrates: 0.4 g; Protein: 6.3 g; Fat: 4.8 g; Sugar: 0.2 g; Sodium: 71 mg; Fiber: 0 g

Simple Air-Baked Eggs

Serves: 4, Preparation Time: 5 minutes, Cooking Time: 15 minutes

Ingredients
- 4 large eggs, beaten
- 1 tablespoon olive oil
- 4 teaspoon coconut milk
- 1 tablespoon butter
- ¼ cup spinach
- Salt and pepper to taste
- Cooking spray

Instructions
1. Preheat the air fryer at 350^{0}F for 5 minutes.
2. Mix all ingredients in a mixing bowl.

3. Pour the mixture in a greased baking dish that will fit in the air fryer.
4. Cook for 15 minutes at 350^{0}F.
5. Serve and enjoy!

Nutrition information:

Calories per serving: 139; Carbohydrates: 0.9 g; Protein: 6.8 g; Fat: 12 g; Sugar: 0.3 g; Sodium: 103 mg; Fiber: 0.3 g

Bacon and Eggs Breakfast Frittata

Serves: 4, Preparation Time: 5 minutes, Cooking Time: 15 minutes

Ingredients

- 6 large eggs, beaten
- 6 pieces uncured bacon, fried and crumbled
- 1 tablespoon chives
- Salt and pepper to taste
- Cooking spray

Instructions

1. Preheat the air fryer at 350^{0}F for 5 minutes.
2. Mix all ingredients in a mixing bowl.
3. Pour the mixture in a greased baking dish that will fit in the air fryer.
4. Cook for 15 minutes at 350^{0}F.
5. Serve and enjoy!

Nutrition information:

Calories per serving: 153; Carbohydrates: 0.6 g; Protein: 14 g; Fat: 10.3 g; Sugar: 0.3 g; Sodium: 302 mg; Fiber: 0 g

Air Fried Quiche

Serves: 8, Preparation Time: 10 minutes, Cooking Time: 20 minutes

Ingredients

- ½ cup almond flour
- 2 tablespoons heart-healthy oil
- 4 large eggs, beaten
- ¼ cup unsweetened coconut cream
- ½ medium onion, chopped
- ½ cup mushroom, sliced
- 1 tablespoon chives, chopped
- Salt and pepper to taste

Instructions

1. Preheat the air fryer at 350°F for 5 minutes.
2. In a mixing bowl, combine the almond flour and heart-healthy oil.
3. Press the almond flour mixture at the bottom of a heatproof baking dish.
4. Place in the air fryer and cook for 5 minutes.
5. Meanwhile, combine the rest of the ingredients in a mixing bowl.
6. Take the crust out and pour over the egg mixture.
7. Put the baking dish back into the air fryer and cook for 15 minutes at 350°F.
8. Serve and enjoy!

Nutrition information:

Calories per serving: 130; Carbohydrates: 3.5 g; Protein: 5.1 g; Fat: 11.1 g; Sugar: 1.1 g; Sodium: 37 mg; Fiber: 1.6 g

Spanish Frittata

Serves: 6, Preparation Time: 5 minutes, Cooking Time: 15 minutes

Ingredients

- 3 large eggs, beaten
- 2 tablespoons olive oil
- 4 ounces cooked Mexican chorizo sausage, sliced
- ½ medium zucchini, sliced
- A dash of oregano
- A dash of Spanish paprika
- Cooking spray

Instructions

1. Preheat the air fryer at 350^0F for 5 minutes.
2. Combine all ingredients in a mixing bowl until well combined.
3. Pour into a greased baking dish that will fit in the air fryer basket.
4. Place the baking dish in the air fryer.
5. Cook for 15 minutes at 350^0F.
6. Serve and enjoy!

Nutrition information:

Calories per serving: 165; Carbohydrates: 1.2 g; Protein: 8 g; Fat: 14.2 g; Sugar: 0.4 g; Sodium: 270 mg; Fiber: 0.3 g

Air Fried Shirred Eggs

Serves: 4, Preparation Time: 8 minutes, Cooking Time: 15 minutes

Ingredients

- 4 large eggs, beaten
- 2 tablespoons coconut cream
- 2 tablespoons butter, unsalted
- 2 teaspoon fresh chives, chopped
- Salt and pepper to taste
- 2 ounces uncured ham, chopped
- 1 egg, whole
- Cooking spray

Instructions

1. Preheat the air fryer at 350^{0}F for 5 minutes.
2. In a mixing bowl, combine the beaten eggs, coconut cream, butter, and chives. Season with salt and pepper to taste.
3. Pour into a greased baking dish that will fit in the air fryer and sprinkle ham on top.
4. Crack 1 egg on top.
5. Place in the air fryer and cook for 15 minutes at 350^{0}F.
6. Serve and enjoy!

Nutrition information:

Calories per serving: 171; Carbohydrates: 1.4 g; Protein: 10.8 g; Fat: 13.5 g; Sugar: 1.1 g; Sodium: 234 mg; Fiber: 0 g

Air Fryer Tofu

Serves: 3, Preparation Time: 12 hours, Cooking Time: 10 minutes

Ingredients
- 1 block Fresh tofu, cut into cubes
- 2 tablespoons low-sodium soy sauce
- 4 tablespoons olive oil
- 1 teaspoon turmeric powder
- ½ teaspoon garlic powder

Instructions
1. In a mixing bowl, combine the tofu, soy sauce, 3 tablespoons of olive oil, turmeric, and garlic powder.
2. Marinate in the fridge overnight or until the tofu cubes have absorbed the marinade.
3. Preheat the air fryer at 350°F for 5 minutes.
4. Before putting the tofu cubes in the air fryer basket, drizzle with the remaining olive oil.
5. Place in the fryer basket and cook for 10 minutes at 350°F.
6. Serve and enjoy!

Nutrition information:
Calories per serving: 295; Carbohydrates: 3.3 g; Protein: 16.3 g; Fat: 26 g; Sugar: 1.2 g; Sodium: 348 mg; Fiber: 1.9 g

Easy Breakfast Frittata

Serves: 3, Preparation Time: 5 minutes, Cooking Time: 20 minutes

Ingredients

- 3 tablespoons olive oil
- 3 cloves of garlic, minced
- 1 medium onion, chopped
- ½ pound ground beef (85% lean, 15% fat)
- 3 eggs, beaten
- Salt and pepper to taste

Instructions

1. Heat oil in a skillet under medium heat.
2. Sauté the garlic and onion until fragrant.
3. Add the ground beef and sauté for 5 minutes or until lightly golden. Set aside.
4. Preheat the air fryer at 320^0F for 5 minutes.
5. In a mixing bowl, combine the rest of the ingredients.
6. Place the sautéed beef in a greased baking dish that will fit in the air fryer chamber.
7. Pour over the egg mixture.
8. Cook for 20 minutes at 320^0F.
9. Serve and enjoy!

Nutrition information:

Calories per serving: 415; Carbohydrates: 4.7 g; Protein: 27.3 g; Fat: 31.3 g; Sugar: 1.7 g; Sodium: 142 mg; Fiber: 0.5g

Baked Spinach Omelet

Serves: 4, Preparation Time: 5 minutes, Cooking Time: 15 minutes

Ingredients

- 4 large eggs, beaten
- ¼ cup coconut milk
- 2 tablespoons olive oil
- 1 tablespoon melted butter
- 8 ounces baby spinach, chopped finely
- Salt and pepper to taste
- Cooking spray

Instructions

1. Preheat the air fryer at 350^{0}F for 5 minutes.
2. In a mixing bowl, combine the eggs, coconut milk, olive oil, and butter until well combined.
3. Add the spinach and season with salt and pepper to taste.
4. Pour all ingredients in a greased baking dish that will fit in the air fryer.
5. Bake at 350^{0}F for 15 minutes.
6. Serve and enjoy!

Nutrition information:

Calories per serving: 198; Carbohydrates: 3 g; Protein: 8.3 g; Fat: 23.3 g; Sugar: 0.4 g; Sodium: 136 mg; Fiber: 1.4 g

Turkey and Kale Casserole

Serves: 4, Preparation Time: 5 minutes, Cooking Time: 15 minutes

Ingredients
- 4 large eggs, beaten
- 1 cup coconut milk
- ½ teaspoon garlic powder
- ½ teaspoon onion powder
- Salt and pepper to taste
- 1-pound leftover turkey, shredded
- 2 cups kale, chopped
- Cooking spray

Instructions
1. Preheat the air fryer at 350^0F for 5 minutes.
2. In a mixing bowl, combine the eggs, coconut milk, garlic powder, and onion powder. Season with salt and pepper to taste.
3. Place the turkey meat and kale in a greased baking dish.
4. Pour over the egg mixture.
5. Place in the air fryer.
6. Cook for 15 minutes at 350^0F.
7. Serve and enjoy!

Nutrition information:
Calories per serving: 418; Carbohydrates: 6.3 g; Protein: 41.3 g; Fat: 25.5 g; Sugar: 1 g; Sodium: 211 mg; Fiber: 1.4 g

Breakfast Soufflé

Serves: 2, Preparation Time: 5 minutes, Cooking Time: 15 minutes

Ingredients

- 2 large eggs
- 2 tablespoons coconut cream
- Salt and pepper to taste
- A dash of Spanish paprika
- Cooking spray

Instructions

1. Preheat the air fryer at 350°F for 5 minutes.
2. Place the eggs and coconut cream in a bowl. Season with salt and pepper to taste then whisk until fluffy.
3. Pour into greased ramekins and sprinkle with Spanish paprika.
4. Place in the air fryer.
5. Bake for 15 minutes at 350°F.
6. Serve and enjoy!

Nutrition information:

Calories per serving: 103; Carbohydrates: 0.9 g; Protein: 6.5 g; Fat: 8 g; Sugar: 0.4 g; Sodium: 75 mg; Fiber: 0.1 g

Spinach and Egg Spinach Casserole

Serves: 6, Preparation Time: 5 minutes, Cooking Time: 20 minutes

Ingredients
- 4 large eggs, beaten
- 3 large egg whites, beaten
- 3 cups frozen chopped spinach, thawed
- 1 cup mushrooms, sliced
- ½ cup red onion, chopped
- 1 red bell pepper, seeded and julienned
- Salt and pepper to taste
- Cooking spray

Instructions
1. Preheat the air fryer at 310^0F for 5 minutes.
2. In a mixing bowl, combine the eggs and egg whites. Whisk until fluffy.
3. Place the rest of the ingredients in a greased baking dish and pour over the egg mixture.
4. Place in the air fryer chamber.
5. Cook for 20 minutes at 310^0F.
6. Serve and enjoy!

Nutrition information:

Calories per serving: 110; Carbohydrates: 9.7 g; Protein: 10.8 g; Fat: 4.2 g; Sugar: 3.2 g; Sodium: 168 mg; Fiber: 4.7 g

Keto Mushroom Breakfast Casserole

Serves: 4, Preparation Time: 5 minutes, Cooking Time: 20 minutes

Ingredients

- 8 large eggs, beaten
- 2 tablespoons butter
- 1 cup coconut cream
- ½ cup mushrooms, chopped
- 1 teaspoon onion powder
- Salt and pepper to taste
- Cooking spray

Instructions

1. Preheat the air fryer at 310^0F for 5 minutes.
2. In a mixing bowl, combine the eggs, butter, and coconut cream.
3. Pour in a greased baking dish together with the mushrooms and onion powder.
4. Season with salt and pepper to taste.
5. Place in the air fryer chamber and cook for 20 minutes at 310^0F.
6. Serve and enjoy!

Nutrition information:

Calories per serving: 318; Carbohydrates: 3.8 g; Protein: 13.4 g; Fat: 27.8 g; Sugar: 1.6 g; Sodium: 203 mg; Fiber: 0.5 g

Keto Casserole

Serves: 6, Preparation Time: 5 minutes, Cooking Time: 20 minutes

Ingredients

- 2 tablespoons heart-healthy oil
- 12 large eggs, beaten
- ¼ cup coconut milk
- 1 teaspoon garlic powder
- 1 medium onion, chopped
- Salt and pepper to taste
- 3 cups spinach, chopped
- Cooking spray

Instructions

1. Preheat the air fryer at 310^{0}F for 5 minutes.
2. In a mixing bowl, combine all ingredients except for the spinach. Whisk until well combined.
3. Place the spinach in a greased baking dish and pour over the egg mixture
4. Place in the air fryer chamber and cook for 20 minutes at 310^{0}F.
5. Serve and enjoy!

Nutrition information:

Calories per serving: 232; Carbohydrates: 6.3 g; Protein: 15.7 g; Fat: 16.5 g; Sugar: 1.5 g; Sodium: 207 mg; Fiber: 3.8 g

Snacks and Appetizers

Buffalo Chicken Tenders

Serves: 4, Preparation Time: 10 minutes, Cooking Time: 30 minutes

Ingredients
- 1-pound chicken breasts, cut into thick strips
- Salt and pepper to taste
- 1 cup almond flour
- 1 large egg, beaten
- 3 tablespoons butter
- ¼ cup sugar-free hot sauce
- 1 clove of garlic, minced
- ¼ teaspoon paprika
- ¼ teaspoon cayenne pepper
- 1 teaspoon stevia powder

Instructions
1. Preheat the air fryer at 350^0F for 5 minutes.
2. Season the chicken breasts with salt and pepper to taste.
3. Dredge first in beaten egg then in flour mixture.
4. Arrange neatly in the air fryer basket.
5. Close and cook for 30 minutes at 350^0F.
6. Halfway through the cooking time, shake the air fryer basket to cook evenly.
7. Meanwhile, prepare the sauce by combine the rest of the ingredients. Season the sauce with salt and pepper to taste. Set aside.
8. Once the chicken tenders are cooked, place in a bowl with the sauce and toss to coat.
9. Serve and enjoy!

Nutrition information:
Calories per serving: 447; Carbohydrates: 8 g; Protein: 43 g; Fat: 28 g; Sugar: 1.5 g; Sodium: 543 mg; Fiber: 3.5 g

Hasselback Zucchini

Serves: 3, Preparation Time: 10 minutes, Cooking Time: 20 minutes

Ingredients

- 3 medium zucchini
- 3 tablespoons olive oil
- 4 tablespoons coconut cream
- 1 tablespoon lemon juice
- Salt and pepper to taste
- 3 slices bacon, fried and crumbled

Instructions

1. Preheat the air fryer at 350^0F for 5 minutes.
2. Line up chopsticks on both sides of the zucchini and slice thinly until you hit the stick. Brush the zucchinis with olive oil.
3. Place the zucchini in the air fryer. Bake for 20 minutes at 350^0F.
4. Meanwhile, combine the coconut cream and lemon juice in a mixing bowl. Season with salt and pepper to taste.
5. Once the zucchini is cooked, scoop the coconut cream mixture and drizzle on top.
6. Sprinkle with bacon bits.
7. Serve and enjoy!

Nutrition information:

Calories per serving: 245; Carbohydrates: 6.7 g; Protein: 6.7 g; Fat: 22.3 g; Sugar: 4 g; Sodium: 207 mg; Fiber: 2.2 g

Pesto Stuffed Mushrooms

Serves: 5, Preparation Time: 10 minutes, Cooking Time: 15 minutes

Ingredients
- 1 cup basil leaves
- 1 tablespoon lemon juice, freshly squeezed
- ½ cup pine nuts
- ¼ cup olive oil
- Salt to taste
- ½ cup cream cheese
- 1-pound cremini mushrooms, stalks removed

Instructions
1. Preheat the air fryer at 350^0F for 5 minutes.
2. Place all ingredients except the mushrooms in a food processor.
3. Pulse until fine.
4. Scoop the mixture and place on the side where the stalks were removed.
5. Place the mushrooms in the fryer basket.
6. Close and cook for 15 minutes at 350^0F.
7. Serve and enjoy!

Nutrition information:
Calories per serving: 289; Carbohydrates: 7.2 g; Protein: 5.8 g; Fat: 28.2 g; Sugar: 3 g; Sodium: 80 mg; Fiber: 1.2 g

Asparagus Fries

Serves: 5, Preparation Time: 10 minutes, Cooking Time: 15 minutes

Ingredients

- 2 tablespoons parsley, chopped
- ½ teaspoon garlic powder
- ¼ cup almond flour
- ½ teaspoon smoked paprika
- Salt and pepper to taste
- 10 medium asparagus, stems trimmed
- 2 large eggs, beaten

Instructions

1. Preheat the air fryer at 350^{0}F for 5 minutes.
2. In a mixing bowl, combine the parsley, garlic powder, almond flour, and smoked paprika. Season with salt and pepper to taste.
3. Soak the asparagus in the beaten eggs and then dredge in the almond flour mixture.
4. Place in the air fryer basket.
5. Cook for 15 minutes at 350^{0}F.
6. Serve and enjoy!

Nutrition information:

Calories per serving: 70; Carbohydrates: 3 g; Protein: 4.6 g; Fat: 4.8 g; Sugar: 0.8 g; Sodium: 34 mg; Fiber: 1.5 g

Fat Burger Bombs

Serves: 6, Preparation Time: 2 hours, Cooking Time: 20 minutes

Ingredients

- 12 slices uncured bacon, chopped
- 1 cup almond flour
- 2 eggs, beaten
- ½ pound ground beef
- Salt and pepper to taste
- 3 tablespoons olive oil

Instructions

1. In a mixing bowl, combine all ingredients except for the olive oil.
2. Use your hands to form small balls with the mixture. Place in a baking sheet and allow it to set in the fridge for at least 2 hours.
3. Preheat the air fryer at 350^0F for 5 minutes.
4. Brush the meatballs with olive oil on all sides.
5. Place in the air fryer basket.
6. Cook for 20 minutes at 350^0F.
7. Halfway through the cooking time, shake the fryer basket for a more even cooking.
8. Serve and enjoy!

Nutrition information:

Calories per serving: 402; Carbohydrates: 4.5g; Protein: 24 g; Fat: 32.3 g; Sugar: 0.9 g; Sodium: 446 mg; Fiber: 2.3 g

Crispy Keto Pork Bites

Serves: 3, Preparation Time: 2 hours, Cooking Time: 25 minutes

Ingredients

- ½-pound pork belly, sliced to thin strips
- 1 tablespoon butter
- 1 medium onion, diced
- 4 tablespoons coconut cream
- Salt and pepper to taste

Instructions

1. Place all ingredients in a mixing bowl and marinate in the fridge for 2 hours.
2. Preheat the air fryer at 350^0F for 5 minutes.
3. Place the pork strips in the air fryer and bake for 25 minutes at 350^0F.
4. Serve and enjoy!

Nutrition information:

Calories per serving: 307; Carbohydrates: 3.7 g; Protein: 18 g; Fat: 24.3 g; Sugar: 1.7 g; Sodium: 107 mg; Fiber: 0.4 g

Basil Keto Crackers

Serves: 6, Preparation Time: 30 minutes, Cooking Time: 15 minutes

Ingredients

- 1 ¼ cups almond flour
- Salt and pepper to taste
- ½ teaspoon baking powder
- ¼ teaspoon dried basil powder
- A pinch of cayenne pepper powder
- 1 clove of garlic, minced
- 3 tablespoons heart-healthy oil

Instructions

1. Preheat the air fryer at 325^{0}F for 5 minutes.
2. Mix everything in a mixing bowl to create a dough.
3. Transfer the dough on a clean and flat working surface and spread out until 2mm thick. Cut into squares.
4. Place gently in the air fryer basket. Do this in batches if possible.
5. Cook for 15 minutes at 325^{0}F.
6. Serve and enjoy!

Nutrition information:

Calories per serving: 198; Carbohydrates: 5.2 g; Protein: 5 g; Fat: 18.7 g; Sugar: 1 g; Sodium: 0 mg; Fiber: 3 g

Air Fried Kale Chips

Serves: 2, Preparation Time: 5 minutes, Cooking Time: 10 minutes

Ingredients
- 1 bunch kale, chopped into large pieces
- 2 tablespoons olive oil
- 2 tablespoons almond flour
- 1 teaspoon garlic powder
- Salt and pepper to taste

Instructions
1. Preheat the air fryer at 350^{0}F for 5 minutes.
2. In a bowl, combine all ingredients until the kale leaves are coated with the other ingredients.
3. Place in a fryer basket and cook for 10 minutes at 350^{0}F until crispy.
4. Serve and enjoy!

Nutrition information:

Calories per serving: 220; Carbohydrates: 13.5 g; Protein: 5.5 g; Fat: 18 g; Sugar: 2.8 g; Sodium: 46 mg; Fiber: 4.9 g

Bacon Jalapeno Poppers

Serves: 8, Preparation Time: 15 minutes, Cooking Time: 15 minutes

Ingredients

- 4-ounce cream cheese
- ¼ cup cheddar cheese, shredded
- Salt to taste
- 1 teaspoon paprika
- 16 fresh jalapenos, sliced lengthwise and seeds removed
- 16 strips of uncured bacon, cut into half

Instructions

1. Preheat the air fryer at 350^{0}F for 5 minutes.
2. In a mixing bowl, mix together the cream cheese, cheddar cheese, salt, and paprika until well combined.
3. Scoop a teaspoon onto each half of jalapeno peppers.
4. Use a thin strip of bacon and wrap it around the cheese-filled jalapeno half. Wear gloves when doing this step because jalapeno is very spicy.
5. Place in the air fryer basket and cook for 15 minutes at 350^{0}F.
6. Serve and enjoy!

Nutrition information:

Calories per serving: 132; Carbohydrates: 3 g; Protein: 8 g; Fat: 10.1 g; Sugar: 1.8 g; Sodium: 329 mg; Fiber: 0.9 g

Crispy Air Fried Broccoli

Serves: 6, Preparation Time: 5 minutes, Cooking Time: 15 minutes

Ingredients
- ½-pound broccoli, cut into florets
- 2 tablespoons coconut milk
- ¼ teaspoon turmeric powder
- 1 tablespoon almond flour
- Salt and pepper to taste
- 1 teaspoon Garam Masala

Instructions
1. Preheat the air fryer at 350^{0}F for 5 minutes.
2. In a bowl, combine all ingredients until the broccoli florets are coated with the other ingredients.
3. Place in a fryer basket and cook at 350^{0}F for 15 minutes until crispy.
4. Serve and enjoy!

Nutrition information:
Calories per serving: 32; Carbohydrates: 3.5 g; Protein: 1.3 g; Fat: 1.8 g; Sugar: 0.6 g; Sodium: 17 mg; Fiber: 1.5 g

Garlic-Roasted Mushrooms

Serves: 4, Preparation Time: 5 minutes, Cooking Time: 25 minutes

Ingredients
- 2 pounds mushrooms
- 3 tablespoons heart-healthy oil
- ½ teaspoon minced garlic
- Salt and pepper to taste
- 2 teaspoons herbs de Provence

Instructions

1. Preheat the air fryer at 350^{0}F for 5 minutes.
2. Place all ingredients in a baking dish that will fit in the air fryer.
3. Mix to combine.
4. Place the baking dish in the air fryer.
5. Cook for 25 minutes at 350^{0}F.
6. Serve and enjoy!

Nutrition information:

Calories per serving: 158; Carbohydrates: 12.3 g; Protein: 5 g; Fat: 11.8 g; Sugar: 5.3 g; Sodium: 5 mg; Fiber: 5 g

Baked Zucchini Fries

Serves: 6, Preparation Time: 5 minutes, Cooking Time: 15 minutes

Ingredients

*   3 medium zucchinis, sliced into fry sticks
*   2 large egg whites, beaten
*   ½ cup almond flour
*   ¼ teaspoon garlic powder
*   Salt and pepper to taste

Instructions

1. Preheat the air fryer at 425^{0}F for 5 minutes.
2. In a mixing bowl, combine the garlic powder and almond flour. Season with salt and pepper to taste.
3. Soak the zucchini in the beaten eggs and then dredge in the almond flour mixture.
4. Place in the air fryer basket and cook for 15 minutes for 425^{0}F.
5. Serve and enjoy!

Nutrition information:

Calories per serving: 77; Carbohydrates: 5.2 g; Protein: 4.5 g; Fat: 5 g; Sugar: 2.3 g; Sodium: 22 mg; Fiber: 2.3 g

Air Fryer Brussels Sprouts

Serves: 4, Preparation Time: 5 minutes, Cooking Time: 15 minutes

Ingredients

- 2 cups Brussels sprouts, halved
- 2 tablespoons olive oil
- 1 tablespoon balsamic vinegar
- ¼ teaspoon salt

Instructions

1. Preheat the air fryer at 350^0F for 5 minutes.
2. Mix all ingredients in a bowl until the Brussels sprouts are well coated.
3. Place in the air fryer basket.
4. Cook for 15 minutes at 350^0F.
5. Serve and enjoy!

Nutrition information:

Calories per serving: 91; Carbohydrates: 6.3 g; Protein: 2 g; Fat: 7.3 g; Sugar: 2 g; Sodium: 163 mg; Fiber: 2 g

Air Fryer Garlic Chicken Wings

Serves: 4, Preparation Time: 5 minutes, Cooking Time: 25 minutes

Ingredients

- 16 pieces chicken wings
- ¾ cup almond flour
- 2 tablespoons stevia powder
- 4 tablespoons minced garlic
- Salt and pepper to taste
- ¼ cup butter, melted

Instructions

1. Preheat the air fryer at 400^0F for 5 minutes.

2. In a mixing bowl, combine the chicken wings, almond flour, stevia powder, and garlic. Season with salt and pepper to taste.
3. Place in the air fryer basket and cook for 25 minutes at 400^{0}F.
4. Halfway through the cooking time, make sure that you give the fryer basket a shake.
5. Once cooked, place in a bowl and drizzle with melted butter. Toss to coat.
6. Serve and enjoy!

Nutrition information:

Calories per serving: 558; Carbohydrates: 14.5 g; Protein: 28.5 g; Fat: 46 g; Sugar: 0.9 g; Sodium: 1011 mg; Fiber: 2.8 g

Tofu Stuffed Peppers

Serves: 8, Preparation Time: 5 minutes, Cooking Time: 10 minutes

Ingredients
- 1 package firm tofu, crumbled
- 1 medium onion, finely chopped
- 3 tablespoons heart-healthy oil
- ½ teaspoon turmeric powder
- ½ teaspoon red chili powder
- 1 teaspoon coriander powder
- Salt to taste
- 8 banana peppers, top end sliced and seeded

Instructions
1. Preheat the air fryer at 325^{0}F for 5 minutes.
2. In a mixing bowl, combine the tofu, onion, oil, turmeric powder, red chili powder, coriander power, and salt. Mix until well combined.
3. Scoop the tofu mixture into the hollows of the banana peppers.
4. Place the stuffed peppers in the air fryer.
5. Close and cook for 10 minutes at 325^{0}F.
6. Serve and enjoy!

Nutrition information:

Calories per serving: 113; Carbohydrates: 4.6 g; Protein: 6.6 g; Fat: 8.5 g; Sugar: 1.9 g; Sodium: 13.6 mg; Fiber: 2.5 g

Extra Crispy Onion Rings

Serves: 3, Preparation Time: 5 minutes, Cooking Time: 15 minutes

Ingredients

- ½ cup almond flour
- 1 tablespoon baking powder
- 1 tablespoon smoked paprika
- Salt and pepper to taste
- 1 large egg, beaten
- ¾ cup coconut milk
- 1 large white onion, sliced into rings

Instructions

1. Preheat the air fryer at 350°F for 5 minutes.
2. In a mixing bowl, mix the almond flour, baking powder, smoked paprika, salt and pepper.
3. In another bowl, combine the eggs and coconut milk.
4. Soak the onion slices into the egg mixture.
5. Dredge the onion slices in the beaten egg and then in the almond flour mixture.
6. Place in the air fryer basket.
7. Cook for 15 minutes at 350°F.
8. Halfway through the cooking time, shake the fryer basket for even cooking.
9. Serve and enjoy!

Nutrition information:

Calories per serving: 268; Carbohydrates: 11.3 g; Protein: 8 g; Fat: 23.3 g; Sugar: 3.1 g; Sodium: 34 mg; Fiber: 3.7g

Air Fried Mediterranean Vegetables

Serves: 4, Preparation Time: 5 minutes, Cooking Time: 15 minutes

Ingredients
- 1 large zucchini
- 1 green pepper, seeded and julienned
- 1 red pepper, seeded and julienned
- 1 teaspoon mixed herbs
- 1 teaspoon mustard
- 2 teaspoon minced garlic
- ¼ cup olive oil
- Salt and pepper to taste

Instructions
1. Preheat the air fryer at 350^{0}F for 5 minutes.
2. Place all ingredients in a baking dish that will fit in the air fryer.
3. Place in the air fryer.
4. Cook for 15 minutes at 350^{0}F.
5. Serve and enjoy!

Nutrition information:

Calories per serving: 144; Carbohydrates: 5.3 g; Protein: 1 g; Fat: 13.8 g; Sugar: 2.8 g; Sodium: 16 mg; Fiber: 1 g

Old Bay Chicken Wings

Serves: 4, Preparation Time: 5 minutes, Cooking Time: 25 minutes

Ingredients

- 16 pieces chicken wings
- ¾ cup almond flour
- 1 tablespoon old bay spices
- 1 teaspoon lemon juice, freshly squeezed
- Salt and pepper to taste
- ½ cup butter

Instructions

1. Preheat the air fryer at 350^0F for 5 minutes.
2. In a mixing bowl, combine all ingredients except for the butter.
3. Place in the air fryer basket.
4. Cook for 25 minutes at 350^0F.
5. Halfway through the cooking time, shake the fryer basket for even cooking.
6. Once cooked, drizzle with melted butter.
7. Serve and enjoy!

Nutrition information:

Calories per serving: 647; Carbohydrates: 5 g; Protein: 28.8 g; Fat: 58.8 g; Sugar: 1 g; Sodium: 1564 mg; Fiber: 2.8 g

Air Fried Blooming Onion

Serves: 4, Preparation Time: 5 minutes, Cooking Time: 20 minutes

Ingredients

- 1 large white onion
- ¼ cup coconut milk
- 2 large eggs, beaten
- ¾ cup almond flour
- 1 ½ teaspoon paprika
- 1 teaspoon garlic powder
- ½ teaspoon Cajun seasoning
- Salt and pepper to taste
- Cooking spray

Instructions

1. Preheat the air fryer at 350^0F for 5 minutes
2. Peel the onion, cut off the top and make random slices.
3. In a mixing bowl, combine the coconut milk and the eggs.
4. Soak the onion in the egg mixture.
5. In another bowl, combine the almond flour, paprika, garlic powder, Cajun seasoning, salt and pepper.
6. Dredge the onion in the almond flour mixture.
7. Grease the basket with cooking spray.
8. Place in the air fryer basket. Cook for 20 minutes at 350^0F.
9. Serve and enjoy!

Nutrition information:

Calories per serving: 205; Carbohydrates: 9.5 g; Protein: 8.5 g; Fat: 16 g; Sugar: 2.8 g; Sodium: 174 mg; Fiber: 3.5 g

"Soy" And Garlic Mushrooms

Serves: 8, Preparation Time: 2 hours, Cooking Time: 20 minutes

Ingredients

- 2 pounds mushrooms, sliced
- 3 tablespoons olive oil
- 2 cloves of garlic, minced
- ¼ cup coconut aminos

Instructions

1. Place all ingredients in a dish and mix until well combined.
2. Marinate for 2 hours in the fridge.
3. Preheat the air fryer at 350^{0}F for 5 minutes.
4. Place the mushrooms in a heatproof dish that will fit in the air fryer.
5. Cook for 20 minutes at 350^{0}F.
6. Serve and enjoy!

Nutrition information:

Calories per serving: 84; Carbohydrates: 7.8 g; Protein: 2.5 g; Fat: 5.6 g; Sugar: 4.1 g; Sodium: 137 mg; Fiber: 2.5 g

Chicken Recipes

Air Fryer Roasted Garlic Chicken

Serves: 16 , Preparation Time: 5 minutes, Cooking Time: 50 minutes

Ingredients
- 4 pounds whole chicken
- 4 cloves of garlic, minced
- Salt and pepper to taste

Instructions
1. Preheat the air fryer at 330^0F for 5 minutes
2. Season the whole chicken with garlic, salt, and pepper.
3. Place in the air fryer basket.
4. Cook for 30 minutes at 330^0F.
5. Flip the chicken on the other side and cook for another 20 minutes.
6. Serve and enjoy!

Nutrition information:
 Calories per serving: 130; Carbohydrates: 0.3 g; Protein: 14.1 g; Fat: 7.7 g; Sugar: 0 g; Sodium: 42 mg; Fiber: 0 g

Air Fried Chicken

Serves: 4, Preparation Time: 5 minutes, Cooking Time: 30 minutes

Ingredients
- 1 large egg, beaten
- ¼ cup coconut milk
- 4 small chicken thighs

- ½ cup almond flour
- 1 tablespoons old bay Cajun seasoning
- Salt and pepper to taste

Instructions

1. Preheat the air fryer at 350^{0}F for 5 minutes.
2. Mix the egg and coconut milk in a bowl.
3. Soak the chicken thighs in the beaten egg mixture.
4. In a mixing bowl, combine the almond flour, Cajun seasoning, salt and pepper.
5. Dredge the chicken thighs in the almond flour mixture.
6. Place in the air fryer basket.
7. Cook for 30 minutes at 350^{0}F.
8. Serve and enjoy!

Nutrition information:

Calories per serving: 408; Carbohydrates: 4.5 g; Protein: 35.5 g; Fat: 29.3 g; Sugar: 0.7 g; Sodium: 1063 mg; Fiber: 2 g

Air Fried Lemon Pepper Chicken

Serves: 1, Preparation Time:5 minutes, Cooking Time: 25 minutes

Ingredients

- 1 chicken breast
- 2 lemons, sliced and rinds reserved
- Salt and pepper to taste
- 1 teaspoon minced garlic

Instructions

1. Preheat the air fryer at 400^{0}F for 5 minutes.
2. Place all ingredients in a baking dish that will fit in the air fryer.
3. Place in the air fryer basket.
4. Cook for 20 minutes at 400^{0}F.
5. Serve and enjoy!

Nutrition information:

Calories per serving: 223; Carbohydrates: 6.4 g; Protein: 37 g; Fat: 4.3 g; Sugar: 1 g; Sodium: 103 mg; Fiber: 0.5 g

Air Fried Chicken Tikkas

Serves: 4, Preparation Time: 5 minutes, Cooking Time: 50 minutes

Ingredients

- 1-pound chicken
- 1 cup coconut milk
- 1 bell pepper, seeded and julienned
- 1 teaspoon turmeric powder
- 1 teaspoon coriander powder
- 2 tablespoons olive oil
- 1 thumb-size ginger, grated
- 1 teaspoon Garam Masala

Instructions

1. Preheat the air fryer at 350^{0}F for 5 minutes.
2. Place all ingredients in a baking dish that will fit in the air fryer.
3. Stir to combine.
4. Place in the air fryer.
5. Cook for 50 minutes at 350^{0}F.
6. Serve and enjoy!

Nutrition information:

Calories per serving: 315; Carbohydrates: 6.3 g; Protein: 15.8 g; Fat: 26.8 g; Sugar: 1.3 g; Sodium: 51 mg; Fiber: 0.9 g

Flourless Chicken Cordon Bleu

Serves: 1, Preparation Time: 10 minutes, Cooking Time: 30 minutes

Ingredients

- 1 chicken breast, butterflied
- 1 teaspoon parsley
- Salt and pepper to taste
- 1 slice cheddar cheese
- 1 slice of ham
- 1 small egg, beaten
- ¼ cup almond flour

Instructions

1. Preheat the air fryer at 350^0F for 5 minutes.
2. Season the chicken with parsley, salt and pepper to taste.
3. Place the cheese and ham in the middle of the chicken and roll. Secure with toothpick.
4. Soak the rolled-up chicken in egg and dredge in almond flour.
5. Place in the air fryer.
6. Cook for 30 minutes at 350^0F.

Nutrition information:

Calories per serving: 588; Carbohydrates: 8 g; Protein: 64 g; Fat: 33 g; Sugar: 2 g; Sodium: 739 mg; Fiber: 3.7 g

Air Fried KFC Chicken Strips

Serves: 1, Preparation Time: 5 minutes, Cooking Time: 20 minutes

Ingredients

- 1 chicken breast, cut into strips
- 1 large egg, beaten
- Salt and pepper to taste
- A dash of thyme
- A dash of oregano
- A dash of paprika
- 2 tablespoons unsweetened dried coconut
- 2 tablespoons almond flour

Instructions

1. Preheat the air fryer at 425^0F for 5 minutes
2. Soak the chicken in the beaten egg.
3. In a mixing bowl, combine the rest of the ingredients until well combined.
4. Dredge the chicken in the dry ingredients.
5. Place in the air fryer basket.
6. Cook for 20 minutes at 350^0F.
7. Serve and enjoy!

Nutrition information:

Calories per serving: 423; Carbohydrates: 6.5 g; Protein: 47 g; Fat: 23 g; Sugar: 1.6 g; Sodium: 164 mg; Fiber: 3.8 g

Southern Fried Chicken Tenders

Serves: 4 , Preparation Time: 5 minutes, Cooking Time: 25 minutes

Ingredients
- 4 chicken breasts
- 1 large egg
- ½ teaspoon cayenne pepper
- ½ teaspoon onion powder
- ½ teaspoon garlic powder
- Salt and pepper to taste
- ¼ cup almond flour

Instructions
1. Preheat the air fryer at 350^0F for 5 minutes.
2. Soak the chicken in the beaten egg.
3. Season the chicken breasts with cayenne pepper, onion powder, garlic powder, salt and pepper.
4. Dredge in the almond flour.
5. Place in the air fryer and cook for 25 minutes at 350^0F.
6. Serve and enjoy!

Nutrition information:
Calories per serving: 260; Carbohydrates: 2.3 g; Protein: 40.5 g; Fat: 9 g; Sugar: 0.4 g; Sodium: 107 mg; Fiber: 1 g

Easy Southern Chicken

Serves: 6, Preparation Time: 5 minutes, Cooking Time: 30 minutes

Ingredients
- 3-pounds chicken quarters
- 1 teaspoon salt

- 1 teaspoon pepper
- 1 teaspoon garlic powder
- 1 teaspoon paprika
- 1 cup coconut flour

Instructions

1. Preheat the air fryer at 350^{0}F for 5 minutes.
2. Combine all ingredients in a bowl. Give a good stir.
3. Place ingredients in the air fryer.
4. Cook for 30 minutes at 350^{0}F.
5. Serve and enjoy!

Nutrition information:

Calories per serving: 526; Carbohydrates: 4.3 g; Protein: 55.7 g; Fat: 30.8 g; Sugar: 1.2 g; Sodium: 616 mg; Fiber: 2.8 g

Keto Air Fryer Tandoori Chicken

Serves: 4, Preparation Time: 2 hours, Cooking Time: 20 minutes

Ingredients

- 1-pound chicken tenders, cut in half
- ½ cup coconut milk
- 1 tablespoon grated ginger
- 1 tablespoon minced garlic
- ¼ cup cilantro leaves, chopped
- 1 teaspoon turmeric
- 1 teaspoon Garam Masala
- 1 teaspoon smoked paprika
- Salt and pepper to taste

Instructions

1. Place all ingredients in a bowl and stir to coat the chicken with all ingredients.
2. Marinate in the fridge for 2 hours.

3. Preheat the air fryer at 400⁰F for 5 minutes.
4. Place the chicken pieces in the air fryer basket.
5. Cook for 20 minutes at 400⁰F.
6. Serve and enjoy!

Nutrition information:

Calories per serving: 255; Carbohydrates: 3.3 g; Protein: 36 g; Fat: 10.3 g; Sugar: 0.2 g; Sodium: 90 mg; Fiber: 0.6 g

Crispy Coconut Air Fried Chicken

Serves: 4, Preparation Time: 5 minutes, Cooking Time: 25 minutes

Ingredients
- 1-pound chicken tenderloins
- ¼ cup olive oil
- ¼ cup coconut flour
- Salt and pepper to taste
- ½ teaspoon ground cumin
- ½ teaspoon smoked paprika
- ½ teaspoon garlic powder
- ½ teaspoon onion powder

Instructions
1. Preheat the air fryer at 325⁰F for 5 minutes.
2. Soak the chicken tenderloins in olive oil.
3. Mix the rest of the ingredients and stir using your hands to combine everything.
4. Place the chicken pieces in the air fryer basket.
5. Cook for 25 minutes at 325⁰F.
6. Serve and enjoy!

Nutrition information:

Calories per serving: 353; Carbohydrates: 2.8 g; Protein: 36 g; Fat: 21.5 g; Sugar: 0.5 g; Sodium: 88 mg; Fiber: 1.2 g

Air Fried Chicken Drumsticks

Serves: 3, Preparation Time: 5 minutes, Cooking Time: 30 minutes

Ingredients
- 6 chicken drumsticks
- ½ cup coconut milk
- ½ cup almond flour
- ½ teaspoon salt
- ½ teaspoon paprika
- ½ teaspoon oregano
- 3 tablespoons melted butter

Instructions
1. Preheat the air fryer at 225^0F for 5 minutes.
2. Soak the chicken drumsticks in coconut milk.
3. In a mixing bowl, combine the almond flour, salt, paprika, and oregano.
4. Dredge the chicken in the almond flour mixture.
5. Place the chicken pieces in the air fryer basket.
6. Air fry for 30 minutes at 325^0F.
7. Halfway through the cooking time, give the fryer basket a shake.
8. Drizzle with melted butter once cooked.
9. Serve and enjoy!

Nutrition information:
Calories per serving: 461; Carbohydrates: 8 g; Protein: 10.5 g; Fat: 31.5 g; Sugar: 1 g; Sodium: 695 mg; Fiber: 2.8 g

Air Fried Lemon Chicken

Serves: 4, Preparation Time: 5 minutes, Cooking Time: 30 minutes

Ingredients

- 4 boneless chicken breasts
- 3 tablespoons olive oil
- 1 tablespoon Spanish paprika
- 2 tablespoons lemon juice, freshly squeezed
- 1 tablespoon stevia powder
- 2 teaspoon minced garlic
- Salt and pepper to taste

Instructions

1. Preheat the air fryer at 325^0F for 5 minutes.
2. Place all ingredients in a baking dish that will fit in the air fryer. Stir to combine.
3. Place the chicken pieces in the air fryer.
4. Cook for 30 minutes at 325^0F.
5. Serve and enjoy!

Nutrition information:

Calories per serving: 296; Carbohydrates: 1.9 g; Protein: 37.5 g; Fat: 14.8 g; Sugar: 0.3 g; Sodium: 92 mg; Fiber: 0.7 g

Keto Chicken Pot Pie

Serves: 6, Preparation Time: 5 minutes, Cooking Time: 30 minutes

Ingredients

- 2 tablespoons butter
- ½ cup broccoli, chopped
- ¼ small onion, chopped
- 2 cloves of garlic, minced
- ¾ cup coconut milk
- 1 cup chicken broth
- 1-pound chicken, cooked, shredded
- Salt and pepper to taste
- 4 ½ tablespoons butter, melted
- 1/3 cup coconut flour
- 4 large eggs

Instructions

1. Preheat the air fryer at 325^{0}F for 5 minutes.
2. Place 2 tablespoons butter, broccoli, onion, garlic, coconut milk, chicken broth, and chicken in a baking dish that will fit in the air fryer. Season with salt and pepper to taste.
3. In a mixing bowl, combine the butter, coconut flour, and eggs.
4. Sprinkle evenly on top of the chicken and broccoli mixture.
5. Place the dish in the air fryer.
6. Cook for 30 minutes at 325^{0}F.
7. Serve and enjoy!

Nutrition information:

Calories per serving: 383; Carbohydrates: 4 g; Protein: 29 g; Fat: 28 g; Sugar: 1 g; Sodium: 367 mg; Fiber: 1.4 g

Crack Chicken

Serves: 4, Preparation Time: 10 minutes, Cooking Time: 25 minutes

Ingredients

- 4 chicken breasts
- ¼ cup olive oil
- 1 block cream cheese
- Salt and pepper to taste
- 8 slices of bacon, fried and crumbled

Instructions

1. Preheat the air fryer at 350^0F for 5 minutes.
2. Place the chicken breasts in a baking dish that will fit in the air fryer.
3. Spread the olive oil, cream cheese and crumbled bacon on top of the chicken. Season with salt and pepper to taste.
4. Place the baking dish with the chicken and cook for 25 minutes at 350^0F.
5. Serve and enjoy!

Nutrition information:

Calories per serving: 624; Carbohydrates: 3.5 g; Protein: 48.5 g; Fat: 455 g; Sugar: 2.1 g; Sodium: 655 mg; Fiber: 0 g

Chicken Picatta

Serves: 8, Preparation Time: 5 minutes, Cooking Time: 35 minutes

Ingredients

- 2 pounds chicken thighs
- 1 cup almond flour
- 4 tablespoons butter
- 3 tablespoons olive oil
- 1 medium onion, diced

- ½ cup chicken stock
- Juice from 2 lemons, freshly squeezed
- 2 tablespoons capers
- Salt and pepper to taste
- 1 large egg, beaten

Instructions

1. Preheat the air fryer at 325^{0}F for 5 minutes.
2. Combine all ingredients in a baking dish. Make sure that all lumps are removed.
3. Place the baking dish in the air fryer chamber.
4. Cook for 35 minutes at 325^{0}F.
5. Serve and enjoy!

Nutrition information:

Calories per serving: 441; Carbohydrates: 5.4 g; Protein: 31.1 g; Fat: 34.3 g; Sugar: 1.6 g; Sodium: 326 mg; Fiber: 2 g

French Garlic Chicken

Serves: 4, Preparation Time: 2 hours, Cooking Time: 25 minutes

Ingredients

- 2 teaspoons herbs de Provence
- 2 tablespoon olive oil
- 1 tablespoon Dijon mustard
- 1 tablespoon cider vinegar
- Salt and pepper to taste
- 1-pound chicken thighs

Instructions

1. Place all ingredients in a Ziploc bag.
2. Marinate in the fridge for at least 2 hours.
3. Preheat the air fryer at 350^{0}F for 5 minutes.
4. Place the chicken in the fryer basket.

5. Cook for 25 minutes at 350^{0}F.
6. Serve and enjoy!

Nutrition information:

Calories per serving: 308; Carbohydrates: 0.8 g; Protein: 26.8 g; Fat: 22.5 g; Sugar: 0 g; Sodium: 299 mg; Fiber: 0.4 g

Air Fryer Chicken Balls

Serves: 3, Preparation Time: 2 hours, Cooking Time: 20 minutes

Ingredients
- 2 large eggs, beaten
- 1 tablespoon coconut milk
- 1 ½ teaspoon herbs de Provence
- Salt and pepper to taste
- ¾ pound skinless, boneless chicken breasts, ground
- ½ cup almond flour

Instructions
1. Mix all ingredients in a bowl.
2. Form 1½-inch small balls using the palms of your hands.
3. Place in the fridge to set for at least 2 hours.
4. Preheat the air fryer at 325^{0}F for 5 minutes.
5. Place the chicken balls in the fryer basket.
6. Cook for 20 minutes at 325^{0}F.
7. Halfway through the cooking time, give the fryer basket a shake to cook evenly on all sides.
8. Serve and enjoy!

Nutrition information:

Calories per serving: 382; Carbohydrates: 4.7 g; Protein: 34.7 g; Fat: 26 g; Sugar: 0.9 g; Sodium: 133 mg; Fiber: 2.6 g

Air Fried Chicken Tenderloin

Serves: 4, Preparation Time: 10 minutes, Cooking Time: 15 minutes

Ingredients

- 8 chicken tenderloins
- Salt and pepper to taste
- 1 large egg, beaten
- ½ cup almond flour
- 2 tablespoons heart-healthy oil

Instructions

1. Preheat the air fryer at 375^{0}F for 5 minutes.
2. Season the chicken tenderloin with salt and pepper to taste.
3. Soak in beaten eggs and then dredge in the almond flour.
4. Place in the air fryer and brush with heart-healthy oil.
5. Cook for 15 minutes at 375^{0}F.
6. Halfway through the cooking time, give the fryer basket a shake to cook evenly.
7. Serve and enjoy!

Nutrition information:

Calories per serving: 307; Carbohydrates: 3 g; Protein: 32.5 g; Fat: 18.3 g; Sugar: 0.7 g; Sodium: 85 g; Fiber: 1.8 g

Air Fried Chicken Parm

Serves: 2, Preparation Time: 5 minutes, Cooking Time: 20 minutes

Ingredients

- 6 tablespoons almond flour
- 2 tablespoons parmesan cheese
- 2 chicken breasts
- 1 tablespoon butter, melted

Instructions

1. Preheat the air fryer at 350^0F for 5 minutes.
2. Combine the almond flour and parmesan cheese in a plate.
3. Drizzle the chicken breasts with butter.
4. Dredge in the almond flour mixture.
5. Place in the fryer basket.
6. Cook for 20 minutes at 350^0F.
7. Serve and enjoy!

Nutrition information:

Calories per serving: 392; Carbohydrates: 5 g; Protein: 43 g; Fat: 22 g; Sugar: 0.9 g; Sodium: 225 mg; Fiber: 2.7 g

Air Fried Spicy Chicken

Serves: 4, Preparation Time: 10 minutes, Cooking Time: 25 minutes

Ingredients

- 1-pound chicken
- Salt and pepper to taste
- 2 large eggs
- 1 cup coconut milk
- 1 cup almond flour
- 2 tablespoons paprika
- 1 teaspoon garlic powder
- 1 teaspoon onion powder
- 1 tablespoon cayenne pepper
- ¼ cup vegetable oil

Instructions

1. Preheat the air fryer at 350^{0}F for 5 minutes
2. Season the chicken meat with salt and pepper to taste. Set aside.
3. In a mixing bowl, combine the eggs and coconut milk. Set aside.
4. In another bowl, mix the almond flour, paprika, garlic powder, and onion powder.
5. Soak the chicken meat in the egg mixture then dredge in the flour mixture.
6. Place in the air fryer basket.
7. Cook for 25 minutes at 350^{0}F.
8. Meanwhile, prepare the hot sauce by combining the cayenne pepper and vegetable oil.
9. Drizzle over chicken once cooked.
10. Serve and enjoy!

Nutrition information:

Calories per serving: 632; Carbohydrates: 11 g; Protein: 46 g; Fat: 46.8 g; Sugar: 1.8 g; Sodium: 131 mg; Fiber: 5 g

Beef Recipes

Air Fried Steak

Serves: 4, Preparation Time: 5 minutes, Cooking Time: 15 minutes

Ingredients
- 1.5 pounds rib eye steak
- Salt and pepper to taste
- A dash of rosemary
- ½ tablespoon garlic powder
- 3 tablespoons olive oil

Instructions
1. Place all ingredients in a Ziploc bag and marinate in the fridge for at least 2 hours.
2. Preheat the air fryer at 400^0F for 5 minutes.
3. Place the steak in the air fryer and cook for 15 minutes at 400^0F.
4. Serve hot and enjoy.

Nutrition information:
Calories per serving: 478; Carbohydrates: 0.9 g; Protein: 35.5 g; Fat: 37 g; Sugar: 0 g; Sodium: 83 mg; Fiber: 0.1 g

Air Fried Beef Schnitzel

Serves: 1, Preparation Time: 5 minutes, Cooking Time: 15 minutes

Ingredients
- 2 tablespoons vegetable oil
- ½ cup almond flour

- 4 ounces shoulder steak or topside cut, thinly sliced
- 1 large egg, beaten
- 1 slice of lemon, to serve

Instructions

1. Preheat the air fryer at 350^{0}F for 5 minutes.
2. Mix the oil and almond flour together.
3. Dip the schnitzel into the egg and dredge in the almond flour mixture.
4. Press the almond flour so that it sticks on to the beef.
5. Place in the air fryer and cook for 15 minutes at 350^{0}F.
6. Serve with a slice of lemon. Enjoy!

Nutrition information:

Calories per serving: 952; Carbohydrates: 13 g; Protein: 48 g; Fat: 81 g; Sugar: 2.7 g; Sodium: 131 mg; Fiber: 7 g

Air Fryer Beef Casserole

Serves: 8, Preparation Time: 5 minutes, Cooking Time: 30 minutes

Ingredients

- 1-pound ground beef (85% lean, 15% fat)
- 1 medium onion, chopped
- 3 cloves of garlic, minced
- 3 tablespoons olive oil
- 1 green bell pepper, seeded and chopped
- Salt and pepper to taste
- 12 large eggs, beaten

Instructions

1. Preheat the air fryer at 325^{0}F for 5 minutes.
2. In a baking dish that will fit in the air fryer, mix the ground beef, onion, garlic, olive oil, and bell pepper. Season with salt and pepper to taste.
3. Pour in the beaten eggs and give a good stir.

4. Place the dish with the beef and egg mixture in the air fryer.
5. Bake for 30 minutes at 325^{0}F.
6. Serve and enjoy!

Nutrition information:

Calories per serving: 317; Carbohydrates: 3 g; Protein: 25.1 g; Fat: 22.1 g; Sugar: 1.3 g; Sodium: 159 mg; Fiber: 0.4 g

Air Fried Steak with Oregano

Serves: 4, Preparation Time: 5 minutes, Cooking Time: 15 minutes

Ingredients

- 1-pound beef steak, bones removed
- 3 tablespoons heart-healthy oil
- Salt and pepper to taste
- A dash of oregano

Instructions

1. Place all ingredients in a Ziploc bag and marinate in the fridge for at least 2 hours.
2. Preheat the air fryer at 400^{0}F for 5 minutes.
3. Place the steak in the air fryer and cook for 15 minutes at 400^{0}F.
4. Serve and enjoy!

Nutrition information:

Calories per serving: 408; Carbohydrates: 0 g; Protein: 29.8 g; Fat: 31.5 g; Sugar: 0 g; Sodium: 59 mg; Fiber: 0 g

Beef Pot Pie

Serves: 6, Preparation Time: 10 minutes, Cooking Time: 30 minutes

Ingredients

- 1-pound ground beef
- 1 green bell pepper, julienned
- 1 red bell pepper, julienned
- 1 yellow bell pepper, julienned
- 1 medium onion, chopped
- 2 cloves of garlic, minced
- 4 tablespoons heart-healthy oil
- 1 tablespoon butter
- Salt and pepper to taste
- 1 cup almond flour
- 2 large eggs, beaten

Instructions

1. Preheat the air fryer at 350^{0}F for 5 minutes.
2. In a baking dish that will fit in the air fryer, combine the first 9 ingredients. Mix well then set aside.
3. In a mixing bowl, mix the almond flour and eggs to create a dough.
4. Press the dough over the beef mixture.
5. Place in the air fryer and cook for 30 minutes at 350^{0}F.
6. Serve and enjoy!

Nutrition information:

Calories per serving: 461; Carbohydrates: 9.8 g; Protein: 27.3g; Fat: 35.5 g; Sugar: 3.8 g; Sodium: 110 mg; Fiber: 3.3 g

Perfect Air Fried Roast Beef

Serves: 8, Preparation Time: 5 minutes, Cooking Time: 1 hour

Ingredients

- 2 pounds topside of beef
- 2 medium onions, chopped
- 2 celery stalks, sliced
- 1 garlic clove, minced
- A bunch of fresh herbs of your choice
- Salt and pepper to taste
- 3 tablespoons olive oil
- 1 tablespoon butter

Instructions

1. Preheat the air fryer at 350^0F for 5 minutes.
2. Place all the ingredients in a baking dish that will fit in the air fryer and stir.
3. Place the dish in the air fryer and bake for 1 hour at 350^0F.
4. Serve and enjoy!

Nutrition information:

Calories per serving: 387; Carbohydrates: 3.3 g; Protein: 30.1 g; Fat: 27.5 g; Sugar: 1.4 g; Sodium: 80 mg; Fiber: 0.7g

Air Fried Braised Beef Roast

Serves: 4, Preparation Time: 5 minutes, Cooking Time: 2 hours

Ingredients

- 1-pound beef chuck roast
- 2 tablespoons olive oil
- 1 tablespoon butter
- 1 tablespoon Worcestershire sauce
- 2 cloves of garlic, minced
- 1 medium onion, chopped
- 3 celery stalks, sliced
- 1 teaspoon thyme
- 1 teaspoon rosemary
- 3 cups water

Instructions

1. Preheat the air fryer at 350^0F for 5 minutes.
2. Place all ingredients in a deep baking dish that will fit in the air fryer.
3. Bake for 2 hours at 350^0F.
4. Braise the meat with its sauce every 30 minutes until cooked.
5. Serve and enjoy!

Nutrition information:

Calories per serving: 375; Carbohydrates: 5 g; Protein: 28.8 g; Fat: 27 g; Sugar: 2.2 g; Sodium: 178 mg; Fiber: 0.9 g

Texas Beef Brisket

Serves: 8, Preparation Time: 5 minutes, Cooking Time: 1 hour and 30 minutes

Ingredients

- 2 tablespoons chili powder
- 1 tablespoon garlic powder
- 1 tablespoon onion powder
- 2 teaspoons dry mustard
- 1 bay leaf
- 4 tablespoons olive oil
- 2 pounds beef brisket, trimmed
- Salt and pepper to taste
- 1 ½ cup beef stock

Instructions

1. Preheat the air fryer at 400^{0}F for 5 minutes.
2. Place all ingredients in a deep baking dish that will fit in the air fryer.
3. Bake for 1 hour and 30 minutes at 400^{0}F.
4. Stir the beef after every 30 minutes to soak in the sauce.
5. Serve and enjoy!

Nutrition information:

Calories per serving: 408; Carbohydrates: 3.3 g; Protein: 34.3 g; Fat: 28.1 g; Sugar: 0.5 g; Sodium: 202 mg; Fiber: 1 g

Air Fried Grilled Steak

Serves: 2, Preparation Time: 5 minutes, Cooking Time: 45 minutes

Ingredients

- 8 ounces top sirloin steak
- 2 tablespoons olive oil
- ½ tablespoon garlic powder
- Salt and pepper to taste
- 2 tablespoons butter, melted

Instructions

1. Preheat the air fryer at 350°F for 5 minutes.
2. Season the sirloin steaks with olive oil, garlic powder, salt and pepper.
3. Place the beef in the air fryer basket.
4. Cook for 45 minutes at 350°F.
5. Once cooked, serve with butter. Enjoy!

Nutrition information:

Calories per serving: 505; Carbohydrates: 1.8 g; Protein: 31 g; Fat: 41 g; Sugar: 0 g; Sodium: 157 mg; Fiber: 0.2 g

Barbecued Beef Brisket

Serves: 12, Preparation Time: 5 minutes, Cooking Time: 2 hours

Ingredients

- 1 ½ tablespoons paprika
- 2 teaspoons dry mustard
- 2 teaspoons ground black pepper
- 2 teaspoons salt
- 1 teaspoon onion powder
- 1 teaspoon garlic powder
- 1 teaspoon ground cumin
- ¼ teaspoon cayenne pepper
- 3 pounds brisket roast
- 5 tablespoons olive oil

Instructions

1. Place all ingredients in a Ziploc bag and marinate in the fridge for at least 2 hours.
2. Preheat the air fryer at 350^{0}F for 5 minutes.
3. Place the meat in a baking dish that will fit in the air fryer.
4. Place in the air fryer and cook for 2 hours at 350^{0}F.
5. Serve and enjoy!

Nutrition information:

Calories per serving: 385; Carbohydrates: 1.3 g; Protein: 33 g; Fat: 26.8 g; Sugar: 0.1 g; Sodium: 444 mg; Fiber: 0.5 g

Oven-Braised Corned Beef

Serves: 12, Preparation Time: 5 minutes, Cooking Time: 50 minutes

Ingredients
- 4 cups water
- 3 pounds corned beef brisket, cut into chunks
- 2 tablespoons Dijon mustard
- 1 medium onion, chopped
- Salt and pepper to taste

Instructions
1. Preheat the air fryer at 400^{0}F for 5 minutes.
2. Place all ingredients in a baking dish that will fit in the air fryer.
3. Cook for 50 minutes at 400^{0}F.
4. Serve and enjoy!

Nutrition information:

Calories per serving: 290; Carbohydrates: 1.5 g; Protein: 20.8 g; Fat: 21.6 g; Sugar: 0.4 g; Sodium: 1171mg; Fiber: 0.4 g

Herb-Rubbed Top Round Roast

Serves: 16, Preparation Time: 5 minutes, Cooking Time: 1 hour

Ingredients
- 4 pounds beef top round roast
- 3 tablespoons olive oil
- 4 teaspoons dried oregano
- 4 teaspoons dried thyme
- 2 teaspoons dried rosemary
- Salt and pepper to taste
- 1 teaspoon dry mustard

Instructions

1. Preheat the air fryer at 325^{0}F for 5 minutes.
2. Place all ingredients in a baking dish that will fit in the air fryer.
3. Place the dish in the air fryer and cook for 1 hour at 325^{0}F.
4. Serve and enjoy!

Nutrition information:

Calories per serving: 256; Carbohydrates: 0.5 g; Protein: 34.8 g; Fat: 12.8 g; Sugar: 0 g; Sodium: 47 mg; Fiber: 0.2 g

Air Fried Roast Beef

Serves: 10, Preparation Time: 5 minutes, Cooking Time: 2 hours

Ingredients

- 3 pounds bone-in beef roast
- 1 large onion, quartered
- 1 tablespoons fresh thyme
- 1 tablespoon fresh rosemary
- 3 cups beef broth
- 2 tablespoons Worcestershire sauce
- Salt and pepper to taste
- 4 tablespoons olive oil

Instructions

1. Preheat the air fryer at 325^{0}F for 5 minutes.
2. Place all ingredients in a baking dish that will fit in the air fryer.
3. Place the dish in the air fryer and cook for 2 hours at 325^{0}F.
4. Serve and enjoy!

Nutrition information:

Calories per serving: 403; Carbohydrates: 1.9 g; Protein: 35.1 g; Fat: 27.4 g; Sugar: 0.8 g; Sodium: 358 mg; Fiber: 0.3 g

Rosemary Pepper Beef Rib Roast

Serves: 7, Preparation Time: 5 minutes, Cooking Time: 2 hours

Ingredients
- 3 tablespoons vegetable oil
- 7 ribs, beef rib roast
- 3 tablespoons unsalted butter
- 1 medium shallot, chopped
- 2 cloves of garlic, minced
- 2 cups water
- 3 ounces dried porcini mushrooms
- 4 sprigs of thyme
- Salt and pepper to taste

Instructions
1. Preheat the air fryer at 325^{0}F for 5 minutes.
2. Place all ingredients in a baking dish that will fit in the air fryer.
3. Place the dish in the air fryer and cook for 2 hours at 325^{0}F.
4. Serve and enjoy!

Nutrition information:
Calories per serving: 281; Carbohydrates: 6.6 g; Protein: 11 g; Fat: 23.3 g; Sugar: 1.2 g; Sodium: 119 mg; Fiber: 0.3 g

Peppered Roast Beef with Shallots

Serves: 12, Preparation Time: 5 minutes, Cooking Time: 1 hour and 30 minutes

Ingredients
- 3 tablespoons mixed peppercorns
- 3-pound boneless rib roast
- 4 tablespoons olive oil
- Salt to taste

- 4 medium shallots, chopped
- 2 tablespoons whole grain mustard
- ¼ cup flat-leaf parsley, chopped

Instructions

1. Preheat the air fryer at 325^{0}F for 5 minutes.
2. Place all ingredients in a baking dish that will fit in the air fryer.
3. Place the dish in the air fryer and cook for 1 hour and 30 minutes at 325^{0}F.
4. Serve and enjoy!

Nutrition information:

Calories per serving: 363; Carbohydrates: 3.8 g; Protein: 28.8 g; Fat: 26.2 g; Sugar: 1.2 g; Sodium: 109 mg; Fiber: 1.1 g

Bullet-Proof Beef Roast

Serves: 12, Preparation Time: 2 hours, Cooking Time: 2 hours

Ingredients

- 4 tablespoons olive oil
- Salt and pepper to taste
- 1 cup organic beef broth
- 3 pounds beef round roast

Instructions

1. Place all the ingredients in a Ziploc bag and marinate in the fridge for 2 hours.
2. Preheat the air fryer at 400^{0}F for 5 minutes.
3. Transfer all ingredients in a baking dish that will fit in the air fryer.
4. Place in the air fryer and cook for 2 hours at 400^{0}F.
5. Serve and enjoy!

Nutrition information:

Calories per serving: 288; Carbohydrates: 0 g; Protein: 30.2 g; Fat: 17.8 g; Sugar: 0 g; Sodium: 114 mg; Fiber: 0 g

Garlic Roast Beef

Serves: 12, Preparation Time: 2 hours, Cooking Time: 2 hours

Ingredients

- 3 tablespoons olive oil
- 1 teaspoon thyme leaves, chopped
- 1 teaspoon salt
- 1 teaspoon black pepper
- 3-pound eye of round roast
- 1 cup beef stock
- 1 ½ tablespoon minced garlic
- 3 tablespoons butter

Instructions

1. Place all the ingredients in a Ziploc bag and marinate in the fridge for 2 hours.
2. Preheat the air fryer at 400^{0}F for 5 minutes.
3. Transfer all ingredients in a baking dish that will fit in the air fryer.
4. Place in the air fryer and cook for 2 hours for 400^{0}F.
5. Baste the beef with the sauce every 30 minutes.
6. Serve and enjoy!

Nutrition information:

Calories per serving: 240; Carbohydrates: 0.6 g; Protein: 34 g; Fat: 11.3 g; Sugar: 0.1 g; Sodium: 333 mg; Fiber: 0 g

Italian Beef Roast

Serves: 10, Preparation Time: 5 minutes, Cooking Time: 3 hours

Ingredients

- 2 ½ pounds beef round roast
- 1 medium onion, sliced thinly
- 4 tablespoons olive oil
- ½ cup water
- 1 teaspoon basil
- ½ teaspoon thyme
- 1 teaspoon salt
- ¼ teaspoon black pepper

Instructions

1. Preheat the air fryer at 400^{0}F for 5 minutes
2. Place all ingredients in a baking dish and make sure that the entire surface of the beef is coated with spices.
3. Place the baking dish with the beef in the air fryer.
4. Cook for 3 hours at 400^{0}F.
5. Serve and enjoy!

Nutrition information:

Calories per serving: 299; Carbohydrates: 1 g; Protein: 30.1 g; Fat: 18.6 g; Sugar: 0.5 g; Sodium: 273 mg; Fiber: 0.2 g

Balsamic Roast Beef

Serves: 12, Preparation Time: 5 minutes, Cooking Time: 2 hours

Ingredients

- 3 pounds boneless roast beef
- 1 cup organic beef broth
- ½ cup balsamic vinegar
- 4 tablespoons olive oil
- 1 tablespoon coconut aminos
- 1 tablespoon Worcestershire sauce
- 1 tablespoon honey
- ½ teaspoon red pepper flakes
- 4 cloves of garlic, minced

Instructions

1. Preheat the air fryer at 400^0F for 5 minutes
2. Place all ingredients in a baking dish and make sure that the entire surface of the beef is coated with the spices.
3. Place the baking dish with the beef in the air fryer.
4. Cook for 2 hours at 400^0F.
5. Serve and enjoy!

Nutrition information:

Calories per serving: 402; Carbohydrates: 4.2 g; Protein: 34.5 g; Fat: 26.3 g; Sugar: 3.4 g; Sodium: 170 mg; Fiber: 0 g

Roast Beef with Garlic Mustard Crust

Serves: 12, Preparation Time: 5 minutes, Cooking Time: 2 hours

Ingredients

- 4 cloves of garlic, chopped
- 2 cups almond flour
- ¼ cup freshly parsley, chopped
- Salt and pepper to taste
- ¼ cup unsalted butter
- 2 tablespoons olive oil
- 3 pounds boneless beef eye round roast
- ¼ cup Dijon mustard
- 3 ½ cups beef broth

Instructions

1. In a mixing bowl, combine the garlic, almond flour, parsley, salt and pepper.
2. Heat a butter and olive oil in a skillet and brown the beef on all sides.
3. Rub the almond flour mixture all over the beef.
4. Brush with Dijon mustard.
5. Preheat the air fryer at 400^{0}F for 5 minutes
6. Place the crusted beef in a baking dish.
7. Pour beef broth slowly on the beef.
8. Place the baking dish with the beef in the air fryer.
9. Cook for 2 hours at 400^{0}F.
10. Baste the beef with the sauce every 30 minutes.
11. Serve and enjoy!

Nutrition information:

Calories per serving: 352; Carbohydrates: 4.8 g; Protein: 38.7 g; Fat: 20.8 g; Sugar: 0.8 g; Sodium: 474 mg; Fiber: 2.6 g

Seafood Recipes

Air Fried Catfish

Serves: 4, Preparation Time: 5 minutes, Cooking Time: 15 minutes

Ingredients
- 4 catfish fillets
- Salt and pepper to taste
- 1 large egg, beaten
- ¼ cup almond flour
- 4 tablespoons olive oil

Instructions
1. Preheat the air fryer at 350^{0}F for 5 minutes.
2. Season the catfish fillets with salt and pepper to taste.
3. Soak in the beaten eggs and dredge in almond flour.
4. Brush the surface with olive oil
5. Place in the air fryer and cook for 15 minutes at 350^{0}F.
6. Serve and enjoy!

Nutrition information:

Calories per serving: 384; Carbohydrates: 1.6 g; Protein: 29.5 g; Fat: 28.5 g; Sugar: 0.4 g; Sodium: 188 mg; Fiber: 0.9 g

Air Fried Shrimp

Serves: 4, Preparation Time: 5 minutes, Cooking Time: 10 minutes

Ingredients
- 1-pound raw shrimp, peeled and deveined
- ½ cup almond flour

- 1 tablespoon yellow mustard
- 3 tablespoons olive oil
- Salt and pepper to taste

Instructions
1. Preheat the air fryer at 400^{0}F for 5 minutes
2. Place all ingredients in a Ziploc bag and give a good shake.
3. Take the ingredients out of the Ziploc bag.
4. Place in the air fryer basket and cook for 10 minutes at 400^{0}F.
5. Cool about 3 minutes, then take the shrimp from Ziploc bag
6. Serve on the plate and enjoy.

Nutrition information:

Calories per serving: 308; Carbohydrates: 5 g; Protein: 29 g; Fat: 19.3 g; Sugar: 0.7 g; Sodium: 1115 mg; Fiber: 1.9 g

Lemon Fish Fillet

Serves: 4, Preparation Time: 5 minutes, Cooking Time: 15 minutes

Ingredients
- 4 salmon fish fillets
- 1 lemon
- Salt and pepper to taste
- 2 tablespoons vegetable oil
- 1 large egg, beaten
- ½ cup almond flour

Instructions
1. Preheat the air fryer at 400^{0}F for 5 minutes
2. Season the salmon fish fillets with vegetable oil, lemon, salt, and pepper.
3. Soak in the beaten egg and dredge in almond flour.
4. Place in the air fryer basket.
5. Cook for 15 minutes at 400^{0}F.
6. Serve and enjoy!

Nutrition information:

Calories per serving: 628; Carbohydrates: 3.5 g; Protein: 54.8 g; Fat: 43 g; Sugar: 0.8 g; Sodium: 158 mg; Fiber: 1.8 g

Air Fried Cajun Salmon

Serves: 1, Preparation Time: 5 minutes, Cooking Time: 15 minutes

Ingredients

- 1 salmon fillet
- 1 dash of Cajun seasoning mix
- 1 teaspoon juice from lemon, freshly squeezed
- Salt and pepper to taste
- 1 tablespoons extra virgin olive oil

Instructions

1. Preheat the air fryer at 325^{0}F for 5 minutes
2. Place all ingredients in a bowl and toss to coat.
3. Place the fish fillet in the air fryer basket.
4. Bake for 15 minutes at 325^{0}F.
5. Once cooked drizzle with olive oil.
6. Serve and enjoy!

Nutrition information:

Calories per serving: 588; Carbohydrates: 0.4 g; Protein: 50 g; Fat: 42 g; Sugar: 0.1 g; Sodium: 275 mg; Fiber: 0.1 g

Cajun Shrimp

Serves: 2, Preparation Time: 5 minutes, Cooking Time: 8 minutes

Ingredients

- ½-pound raw shrimp, peeled and deveined
- ¼ teaspoon cayenne pepper
- ½ teaspoon old bay seasoning
- ¼ teaspoon smoked paprika
- 3 tablespoons olive oil

Instructions

1. Preheat the air fryer at 390^{0}F for 5 minutes.
2. Toss all ingredients in a bowl that will fit the air fryer.
3. Place the shrimp in the air fryer basket and cook for 8 minutes at 390^{0}F.
4. Serve and enjoy!

Nutrition information:

Calories per serving: 316; Carbohydrates: 2.2 g; Protein: 26 g; Fat: 22.5 g; Sugar: 0 g; Sodium: 1228 mg; Fiber: 0.2 g

Air Fried Hot Prawns

Serves: 2, Preparation Time: 5 minutes, Cooking Time: 5 minutes

Ingredients

- 1 teaspoon chili flakes
- 1 teaspoon chili powder
- ½ teaspoon salt
- ½ teaspoon ground black pepper
- 12 raw prawns, peeled and deveined
- 3 tablespoons olive oil

Instructions

1. Preheat the air fryer at 400°F for 5 minutes.
2. Toss all ingredients in a bowl that will fit the air fryer.
3. Place the prawns in the air fryer basket and cook for 5 minutes at 400°F.
4. Serve and enjoy!

Nutrition information:

Calories per serving: 222; Carbohydrates: 1.7 g; Protein: 7 g; Fat: 21 g; Sugar: 0.2 g; Sodium: 905 mg; Fiber: 0.7 g

Coconut Crusted Prawns

Serves: 3, Preparation Time: 5 minutes, Cooking Time: 6 minutes

Ingredients

- 12 large raw prawns, peeled and deveined
- Salt and pepper to taste
- 1 cup egg white
- 1 cup dried unsweetened coconut
- ½ cup almond flour
- 4 tablespoons butter

Instructions

1. Preheat the air fryer at 400°F for 5 minutes
2. Season the prawns with salt and pepper.
3. Place all ingredients in a Ziploc bag and shake until well combined.
4. Place the ingredients in the air fryer basket.
5. Close and cook for 6 minutes 400°F.
6. Serve and enjoy!

Nutrition information:

Calories per serving: 497; Carbohydrates: 11.7 g; Protein: 19.3g; Fat: 43 g; Sugar: 3.3 g; Sodium: 456 mg; Fiber: 7 g

Hong Kong Style Cod Fish

Serves: 2, Preparation Time: 5 minutes, Cooking Time: 15 minutes

Ingredients

- 2 cod fish fillets
- 1 teaspoon sesame oil
- 1 cup water
- 3 tablespoons coconut aminos
- 3 tablespoons heart-healthy oil
- 5 slices of ginger
- Green onions for garnish

Instructions

1. Preheat the air fryer at 400^0F for 5 minutes.
2. Place all ingredients except for the green onions in a baking dish.
3. Place in the air fryer and cook for 15 minutes at 400^0F.
4. Garnish with green onions.
5. Serve and enjoy!

Nutrition information:

Calories per serving: 418; Carbohydrates: 6 g; Protein: 41.5 g; Fat: 25 g; Sugar: 4.7 g; Sodium: 544 mg; Fiber: 1.6 g

Cod Nuggets

Serves: 3, Preparation Time: 10 minutes, Cooking Time: 20 minutes

Ingredients

- 1 ½ pound cod fillet, cut into big chunks
- Salt and pepper to taste
- 1 egg, beaten
- ½ cup almond flour
- 3 tablespoons olive oil

Instructions

1. Preheat the air fryer at 375^{0}F for 5 minutes.
2. Season the cod fillets with salt and pepper to taste.
3. Add the eggs and mix to combine.
4. Dredge individual cod chunks into the almond flour and set aside on a plate.
5. Brush all sides with olive oil.
6. Place in the fryer basket and cook for 20 minutes at 375^{0}F.
7. Serve and enjoy!

Nutrition information:

Calories per serving: 489; Carbohydrates: 4 g; Protein: 57.7 g; Fat: 26.3 g; Sugar: 0.9 g; Sodium: 201 mg; Fiber: 2.3 g

Crispy Fried Fish Skin

Serves: 2, Preparation Time: 5 minutes, Cooking Time: 10 minutes

Ingredients

- ½ pound salmon skin, patted dry
- Salt and pepper to taste
- 2 tablespoons heart-healthy oil

Instructions

1. Preheat the air fryer at 400^{0}F for 5 minutes.
2. In a large bowl, combine everything and mix well.
3. Place in the fryer basket and close.
4. Cook for 10 minutes at 400^{0}F.
5. Halfway through the cooking time, give a good shake to evenly cook the skin.
6. Serve and enjoy!

Nutrition information:

Calories per serving: 357; Carbohydrates: 0 g; Protein: 25 g; Fat: 28 g; Sugar: 0 g; Sodium: 69 mg; Fiber: 0 g

Air Fried Fish and Zucchini Fries

Serves: 4, Preparation Time: 5 minutes, Cooking Time: 30 minutes

Ingredients

- 1 zucchini, sliced into thick strips
- 1 tablespoon heart-healthy oil
- Salt and pepper to taste
- 2 salmon fish fillets, cut into strips
- Salt and pepper to taste
- 1 large egg, beaten
- 1 cup almond flour
- 1 tablespoon chopped parsley

Instructions

1. Preheat the air fryer at 400^{0}F for 5 minutes.
2. Season the zucchini slices with heart-healthy oil, salt and pepper to taste.
3. Place in the air fryer and fry at 15 minutes at 400^{0}F.
4. Meanwhile, prepare the fish by seasoning the fish fillets with salt and pepper.
5. Soak in beaten egg and dredge in almond flour.
6. Once the fries are done, place the fish in the fryer basket and bake for 20 minutes at 400^{0}F.
7. Garnish with parsley once done. Enjoy!

Nutrition information:

Calories per serving: 453; Carbohydrates: 7.8 g; Protein: 33.3 g; Fat: 2.9 g; Sugar: 2.2 g; Sodium: 90 mg; Fiber: 4 g

Air Fryer Fish Cakes

Serves: 3, Preparation Time: 5 minutes, Cooking Time: 20 minutes

Ingredients

- 1 cup (or 8 oz) cooked salmon, shredded
- 1 cup almond flour
- 2 large eggs, beaten
- Salt and pepper to taste
- 1 tablespoon lemon juice
- 1 tablespoon chopped parsley
- ½ cup dried unsweetened coconut flakes
- 3 tablespoons heart-healthy oil

Instructions

1. Preheat the air fryer at 325^{0}F for 5 minutes
2. Mix the salmon, almond flour, eggs, salt, pepper, lemon juice and parsley in a bowl.
3. Form 2 inches small balls using your hands and dredge in coconut flakes.
4. Brush the surface of the balls with heart-healthy oil.
5. Place in the air fryer basket and cook for 20 minutes at 325^{0}F.
6. Halfway through the cooking time, give the fryer basket a shake.
7. Serve and enjoy!

Nutrition information:

Calories per serving: 638; Carbohydrates: 12 g; Protein: 30 g; Fat: 54.3 g; Sugar: 2.9 g; Sodium: 101 mg; Fiber: 7 g

Air Fried Spicy Lime Fish

Serves: 4, Preparation Time: 5 minutes, Cooking Time: 15 minutes

Ingredients

- 2 salmon fish fillets, cut into pieces
- 1 tablespoon lime juice, freshly squeezed
- 1 teaspoon lime zest
- Salt and pepper to taste
- 1 large egg white, beaten
- 5 tablespoons almond flour
- A dash of chili powder
- 2 tablespoon olive oil

Instructions

1. Preheat the air fryer at 350^{0}F for 5 minutes
2. Place all ingredients in a Ziploc bag and shake until all ingredients are well combined.
3. Take the ingredients out of the Ziploc bag and place in the air fryer basket.
4. Cook for 15 minutes at 400^{0}F.
5. Serve and enjoy!

Nutrition information:

Calories per serving: 350; Carbohydrates: 2.4 g; Protein: 28 g; Fat: 25.3 g; Sugar: 0.5 g; Sodium: 88 mg; Fiber: 1.2 g

Air Fried Fish in Pesto Sauce

Serves: 3, Preparation Time: 5 minutes, Cooking Time: 20 minutes

Ingredients

- ½ cup olive oil
- Salt and pepper to taste
- 1 bunch fresh basil
- 2 cloves of garlic,
- 2 tablespoons pine nuts
- 1 tablespoon parmesan cheese, grated
- 3 white fish fillets

Instructions

1. Preheat the air fryer at 400^{0}F for 5 minutes
2. In a food processor, combine all ingredients except for the fish fillets.
3. Pulse until smooth.
4. Place the fish in a baking dish and pour over the pesto sauce.
5. Place in the air fryer and cook for 20 minutes at 400^{0}F.
6. Serve and enjoy!

Nutrition information:

Calories per serving: 599; Carbohydrates: 1.9 g; Protein: 46.3 g; Fat: 46.3 g; Sugar: 0.2 g; Sodium: 126 mg; Fiber: 0.5 g

Baked Thai Fish

Serves: 4, Preparation Time: 5 minutes, Cooking Time:20 minutes

Ingredients

- 1-pound cod fillet, cut into bite-sized pieces
- ¼ cup coconut milk, freshly squeezed
- Salt and pepper to taste
- 1 tablespoon lime juice, freshly squeezed

Instructions

1. Preheat the air fryer at 325^{0}F for 5 minutes.
2. Place all ingredients in a baking dish that will fit in the air fryer.
3. Place in the air fryer basket.
4. Cook for 20 minutes at 325^{0}F.
5. Serve and enjoy!

Nutrition information:

Calories per serving: 148; Carbohydrates: 0.7 g; Protein: 26.3 g; Fat: 4 g; Sugar: 0 g; Sodium: 27 mg; Fiber: 0 g

Creamy Air Fried Salmon

Serves: 2, Preparation Time: 5 minutes, Cooking Time: 15 minutes

Ingredients

- ½ pound salmon fillet
- Salt and pepper to taste
- 1 teaspoon olive oil
- 1 avocado, pitted and chopped
- ½ clove of garlic
- 2 tablespoons cashew nuts, soaked in water for 10 minutes

Instructions

1. Preheat the air fryer at 400^{0}F for 5 minutes.
2. Season the salmon fillets with salt, pepper, and olive oil.
3. Place in the air fryer basket and cook for 15 minutes at 400^{0}F.
4. Meanwhile, place the rest of the ingredients in a food processor. Season with salt and pulse until smooth.
5. Serve the salmon fillet with the creamy avocado sauce. Enjoy!

Nutrition information:

Calories per serving: 417; Carbohydrates: 9 g; Protein: 27.5 g; Fat: 30.5 g; Sugar: 0.7 g; Sodium: 130 mg; Fiber: 4.9 g

Smoked Trout Frittata

Serves: 6, Preparation Time: 5 minutes, Cooking Time: 15 minutes

Ingredients

- 2 tablespoons olive oil
- 1 medium onion, chopped
- 6 large eggs, beaten
- 16 ounces smoked trout, shredded
- Salt and pepper to taste

Instructions

1. Preheat the air fryer at 400^0F for 5 minutes.
2. Place all ingredients in a mixing bowl until well combined.
3. Pour into a baking dish that will fit in the air fryer.
4. Cook for 15 minutes at 400^0F.
5. Serve and enjoy!

Nutrition information:

Calories per serving: 225; Carbohydrates: 2 g; Protein: 22.5 g; Fat: 20 g; Sugar: 0.9 g; Sodium: 832 mg; Fiber: 0.2 g

Air Fried Cod with Basil Vinaigrette

Serves: 4, Preparation Time: 5 minutes, Cooking Time: 15 minutes

Ingredients

- 4 cod fillets
- Salt and pepper to taste
- Juice from 1 lemon, freshly squeezed
- ¼ cup olive oil
- A bunch of basil, torn

Instructions

1. Preheat the air fryer at 350^{0}F for 5 minutes.
2. Season the cod fillets with salt and pepper to taste.
3. Place in the air fryerand cook for 15 minutes at 350^{0}F.
4. Meanwhile, mix the rest of the ingredients in a bowl and toss to combine.
5. Serve the air-fried cod with the basil vinaigrette. Enjoy!

Nutrition information:

Calories per serving: 200; Carbohydrates: 0.6 g; Protein: 41.5 g; Fat: 2.4 g; Sugar: 0.1 g; Sodium: 143 mg; Fiber: 0.25 g

Fried Fish Nuggets

Serves: 6, Preparation Time: 5 minutes, Cooking Time: 25 minutes

Ingredients

- 1 ½ pounds fresh fish fillet, chopped finely
- 1 teaspoon chili powder
- 1 teaspoon smoked paprika
- 1 tablespoon lemon juice
- Salt and pepper to taste
- 1 cup almond flour
- 1 tablespoon olive oil
- 2 eggs, beaten
- 2 cloves of garlic, minced

Instructions

1. Place all ingredients in a bowl and mix until well combined.
2. Form small nuggets using your hands. Place in the fridge to set for 2 hours.
3. Preheat the air fryer at 350^{0}F for 5 minutes.
4. Carefully place the nuggets in the fryer basket.
5. Cook for 25 minutes at 350^{0}F.
6. Serve and enjoy!

Nutrition information:

Calories per serving: 301; Carbohydrates: 5 g; Protein: 35.8 g; Fat: 16.3 g; Sugar: 1 g; Sodium: 101mg; Fiber: 2.7 g

Air Fried Fish with Coconut Sauce

Serves: 4, Preparation Time: 5 minutes, Cooking Time: 15 minutes

Ingredients

- 1-pound bass fillet
- Salt and pepper to taste
- 1 tablespoon olive oil
- ¼ cup coconut milk
- 2 tablespoons lime juice, freshly squeezed
- 2 tablespoons jalapeno, chopped
- 3 tablespoons parsley, chopped

Instructions

1. Preheat the air fryer at 350^{0}F for 5 minutes.
2. Season the bass with salt and pepper to taste.
3. Brush the surface with olive oil.
4. Place in the air fryer and cook for 15 minutes at 350^{0}F.
5. Meanwhile, place the coconut milk, lime juice, jalapeno and parsley in a saucepan.
6. Heat over medium flame.
7. Serve the fish with the coconut sauce. Enjoy!

Nutrition information:

Calories per serving: 202; Carbohydrates: 1.4 g; Protein: 27.3 g; Fat: 9.3 g; Sugar: 0.3 g; Sodium: 102 mg; Fiber: 0.2 g

Sweets and Desserts

Keto Doughnuts

Serves: 4, Preparation Time: 5 minutes, Cooking Time: 20 minutes

Ingredients
- ¾ cup almond flour
- ¼ cup flaxseed meal
- ¼ cup erythritol
- 1 teaspoon vanilla extract
- 2 large eggs, beaten
- 3 tablespoons heart-healthy oil
- ¼ cup coconut milk
- 1 tablespoon cocoa powder
- Cooking spray

Instructions
1. Place all ingredients in a mixing bowl.
2. Mix until well combined.
3. Scoop the dough into greased, individual doughnut molds.
4. Preheat the air fryer at 350°F for 5 minutes.
5. Cook for 20 minutes at 350°F.
6. Bake in batches if possible.
7. Enjoy!

Nutrition information:
Calories per serving: 329; Carbohydrates: 9.3 g; Protein: 9.5 g; Fat: 29.5 g; Sugar: 1.3 g; Sodium: 48 mg; Fiber: 4.8 g

Baked Chocolate in A Mug

Serves: 8, Preparation Time: 5 minutes, Cooking Time: 15 minutes

Ingredients

- 1 package cream cheese, room temperature
- 4 tablespoons butter
- 1 tablespoon vanilla extract
- ½ cup stevia powder
- ½ cup unsweetened cocoa powder
- 1 cup coconut cream
- Cooking spray

Instructions

1. Preheat the air fryer at 350^0F for 5 minutes.
2. In a mixing bowl, combine all ingredients.
3. Use a hand mixer to mix everything until fluffy.
4. Pour into greased mugs.
5. Place the mugs in the fryer basket.
6. Bake for 15 minutes at 350^0F.
7. Place in the fridge to chill before serving. Enjoy!

Nutrition information:

Calories per serving: 234; Carbohydrates: 19.5 g; Protein: 3.1 g; Fat: 22.3 g; Sugar: 1.7 g; Sodium: 142 mg; Fiber: 1 g

Coconut Cupcake Bites

Serves: 6, Preparation Time: 10 minutes, Cooking Time: 30 minutes

Ingredients

- 1 cup coconut flour
- 1 cup almond milk, unsweetened
- 7 large eggs, beaten
- ½ cup butter
- 1 tablespoon baking powder
- 3 teaspoons vanilla extract
- ½ teaspoon salt
- ¾ cup erythritol
- Cooking spray

Instructions

1. Preheat the air fryer at 350^{0}F for 5 minutes.
2. Mix all ingredients using a hand mixer.
3. Pour into greased, hard cupcake molds.
4. Place in the air fryer basket.
5. Bake for 30 minutes at 350^{0}F or until a toothpick inserted in the middle comes out clean.
6. Bake by batches if possible.
7. Chill before serving. Enjoy!

Nutrition information:

Calories per serving: 350; Carbohydrates: 8.2 g; Protein: 8.8 g; Fat: 31.7 g; Sugar: 3 g; Sodium: 423 mg; Fiber: 2.7 g

Strawberry Shortcake in A Mug

Serves: 4, Preparation Time: 10 minutes, Cooking Time: 25 minutes

Ingredients

- 2/3 cup almond flour
- ½ cup butter
- 3 large eggs, beaten
- 1/3 cup erythritol
- 1 teaspoon vanilla extract
- ¼ teaspoon salt
- ¼ teaspoon liquid stevia
- ½ teaspoon baking powder
- 1 cup strawberries, halved
- Cooking spray

Instructions

1. Preheat the air fryer at 350^{0}F for 5 minutes.
2. In a mixing bowl, combine all ingredients except for the strawberries.
3. Use a hand mixer to mix everything.
4. Pour into greased mugs.
5. Top with sliced strawberries
6. Place the mugs in the fryer basket.
7. Bake for 25 minutes at 350^{0}F.
8. Place in the fridge to chill before serving. Enjoy!

Nutrition information:

Calories per serving: 387; Carbohydrates: 9.3 g; Protein: 9.3 g; Fat: 36 g; Sugar: 3.3 g; Sodium: 84 mg; Fiber: 3.3 g

Cherry Pie Bars

Serves: 12, Preparation Time: 10 minutes, Cooking Time: 35 minutes

Ingredients

- ½ cup butter, softened
- 1 cup erythritol
- ½ teaspoon salt
- 2 large eggs
- ½ teaspoon vanilla
- 1 ½ cups almond flour
- 1 cup fresh cherries, pitted
- ¼ cup water
- 1 tablespoon xanthan gum
- Cooking spray

Instructions

1. Preheat the air fryer at 375^0F for 5 minutes.
2. In a mixing bowl, combine the first 6 ingredients until you form a dough.
3. Press the dough in a greased baking dish that will fit in the air fryer.
4. Place in the air fryer and bake for 10 minutes at 375^0F.
5. Meanwhile, mix the cherries, water, and xanthan gum in a bowl.
6. Take the dough out and pour over the cherry mixture.
7. Return to the air fryer and cook for 25 minutes more at 375^0F.
8. Serve and enjoy!

Nutrition information:

Calories per serving: 177; Carbohydrates: 7 g; Protein: 4.3 g; Fat: 15.5 g; Sugar: 2.4 g; Sodium: 181 mg; Fiber: 2.3 g

Poppy Seed Loaf

Serves: 8, Preparation Time: 10 minutes, Cooking Time: 20 minutes

Ingredients

- 1 ½ cups almond flour
- ¼ cup erythritol powder
- 2 tablespoon psyllium husk powder
- ½ cup coconut milk
- 1/3 cup butter, unsalted
- 2 large eggs, beaten
- 1 ½ teaspoon baking powder
- 2 tablespoons poppy seeds
- ¼ teaspoon vanilla extract
- Cooking spray

Instructions

1. Preheat the air fryer at 350^0F for 5 minutes.
2. In a mixing bowl, combine all ingredients.
3. Use a hand mixer to mix everything.
4. Pour into a greased, small loaf pan that will fit in the air fryer.
5. Bake for 20 minutes at 375^0F or until a toothpick inserted in the middle comes out clean.
6. Serve and enjoy!

Nutrition information:

Calories per serving: 258; Carbohydrates: 8.9 g; Protein: 7.4 g; Fat: 23.4 g; Sugar: 1.1 g; Sodium: 85 mg; Fiber: 4.8 g

Flourless Lemon Bars

Serves: 12, Preparation Time: 5 minutes, Cooking Time: 25 minutes

Ingredients

- ¾ cup coconut milk
- ¼ cup cashews, chopped
- 1 cup dried unsweetened coconut
- 2 tablespoons heart-healthy oil
- ¾ cup erythritol
- 2 eggs, beaten
- ¼ cup fresh lemon juice, freshly squeezed
- 1 teaspoon baking powder
- A dash of salt
- Cooking spray

Instructions

1. Preheat the air fryer at 350°F for 5 minutes.
2. In a mixing bowl, combine all ingredients.
3. Use a hand mixer to mix everything.
4. Pour into a greased baking dish that will fit in the air fryer.
5. Bake for 25 minutes at 350°F or until a toothpick inserted in the middle comes out clean.
6. Serve and enjoy!

Nutrition information:

Calories per serving: 129; Carbohydrates: 4.6 g; Protein: 2.3 g; Fat: 12 g; Sugar: 0.8 g; Sodium: 57 mg; Fiber: 1.3 g

Lava Cake in A Mug

Serves: 3, Preparation Time: 5 minutes, Cooking Time: 15 minutes

Ingredients

- ¼ cup heart-healthy oil
- 1 cup unsweetened dark cocoa powder
- 3 large eggs, beaten
- 2 tablespoons stevia powder
- 1 tablespoon almond flour
- ¼ teaspoon vanilla powder
- Cooking spray

Instructions

1. Preheat the air fryer at 375°F for 5 minutes.
2. Combine all ingredients in a mixing bowl.
3. Grease ramekins with heart-healthy oil and dust with chocolate powder.
4. Pour the batter into the ramekins and place in the fryer basket.
5. Close and bake at 375°F for 15 minutes.
6. Serve and enjoy!

Nutrition information:

Calories per serving: 360; Carbohydrates: 26.3 g; Protein: 12 g; Fat: 27.3 g; Sugar: 0.3 g; Sodium: 71 mg; Fiber: 5.7 g

Keto Hot Buns

Serves: 8, Preparation Time: 8 minutes, Cooking Time: 15 minutes

Ingredients
- 4 large eggs, beaten
- 1 cup coconut milk
- 1/3 cup coconut flour
- 3 tablespoons cacao powder
- ¼ cup cacao nibs
- Cooking spray

Instructions
1. Preheat the air fryer at 375°F for 5 minutes.
2. Combine all ingredients in a mixing bowl.
3. Form buns using your hands and place in a greased baking dish that will fit in the air fryer.
4. Bake for 15 minutes for 375°F.
5. Once air fryer turns off, leave the buns in the air fryer until it cools completely.
6. Serve and enjoy!

Nutrition information:
Calories per serving: 157; Carbohydrates: 4.8 g; Protein: 5.1 g; Fat: 13.6 g; Sugar: 0.4 g; Sodium: 42 mg; Fiber: 1.9 g

Mug Cookie

Serves: 1, Preparation Time: 5 minutes, Cooking Time: 10 minutes

Ingredients

- 1 tablespoon butter
- 3 tablespoons almond flour
- 1 tablespoon erythritol
- A dash of cinnamon
- 1 large egg yolk
- 1/8 teaspoon vanilla extract
- 1 dash of salt
- Cooking spray

Instructions

1. Preheat the air fryer at 375^{0}F for 5 minutes.
2. Combine all ingredients in a mixing bowl.
3. Place in greased mug.
4. Bake in the air fryer for 10 minutes at 375^{0}F.

Nutrition information:

Calories per serving: 308; Carbohydrates: 7.5 g; Protein: 7.3 g; Fat: 27 g; Sugar: 2.2 g; Sodium: 264 mg; Fiber: 2.6 g

Coconut Raspberry

Serves: 8, Preparation Time: 5 minutes, Cooking Time: 20 minutes

Ingredients

- 1 cup coconut milk
- ¼ cup heart-healthy oil
- 3 cups dried unsweetened coconut
- 1/3 cup erythritol powder

- 1 teaspoon vanilla bean
- 1 cup raspberries, blended
- Cooking spray

Instructions

1. Preheat the air fryer at 375^{0}F for 5 minutes.
2. Combine all ingredients in a mixing bowl.
3. Pour into a greased baking dish.
4. Bake in the air fryer for 20 minutes at 375^{0}F.
5. Serve and enjoy!

Nutrition information:

Calories per serving: Carbohydrates: 12 g; Protein: 3 g; Fat: 33.6 g; Sugar: 34 g; Sodium: 28 mg; Fiber: 6.3 g

Dense Vanilla Cake

Serves: 6, Preparation Time: 5 minutes, Cooking Time: 30 minutes

Ingredients

- 1/3 cup water
- ¼ teaspoon salt
- ½ cup erythritol powder
- 2/3 cup butter, melted
- 4 large eggs
- 1 vanilla bean, scraped
- Cooking spray

Instructions

1. Preheat the air fryer at 375^{0}F for 5 minutes.
2. Combine all ingredients in a mixing bowl.
3. Pour into a greased baking dish.
4. Bake in the air fryer for 30 minutes at 375^{0}F.
5. Serve and enjoy!

Nutrition information:

Calories per serving: 233; Carbohydrates: 1.8 g; Protein: 4.5 g; Fat: 23.5 g; Sugar: 0.2 g; Sodium: 316 mg; Fiber: 0 g

Chocolate Chip Mug Cake

Serves: 6, Preparation Time: 5 minutes, Cooking Time: 20 minutes

Ingredients

- 2 ½ cups almond flour
- ¼ cup walnuts, shelled and chopped
- ½ cup butter, unsalted
- 2 large eggs, beaten
- ½ cup erythritol
- ½ cup dark chocolate chips
- ½ teaspoon salt
- ½ teaspoon baking soda
- 1 tablespoon vanilla extract
- Cooking spray

Instructions

1. Preheat the air fryer at 375^{0}F for 5 minutes.
2. Combine all ingredients in a mixing bowl.
3. Place in greased mugs.
4. Bake in the air fryer for 20 minutes at 375^{0}F.
5. Serve and enjoy!

Nutrition information:

Calories per serving: 546; Carbohydrates: 21.2 g; Protein: 13.5 g; Fat: 47.3 g; Sugar: 9.3 g; Sodium: 354 mg; Fiber: 7.2 g

Lime Coconut Bars

Serves: 4, Preparation Time: 5 minutes, Cooking Time: 20 minutes

Ingredients
- ¾ cup coconut flour
- ¼ cup almond flour
- 1 ¼ cup erythritol powder
- ¼ teaspoon salt
- ¼ cup heart-healthy oil
- 4 large eggs
- ½ cup lime juice
- 1 tablespoon lime zest
- ¼ cup dried unsweetened coconut
- Cooking spray

Instructions
1. Preheat the air fryer at 375^{0}F for 5 minutes.
2. Combine all ingredients in a mixing bowl.
3. Place in greased mug.
4. Bake in the air fryer for 20 minutes at 375^{0}F.
5. Serve and enjoy!

Nutrition information:
Calories per serving: 458; Carbohydrates: 17.5 g; Protein: 10 g; Fat: 40.8 g; Sugar: 3.5 g; Sodium: 269 mg; Fiber: 5.8 g

Macaroon Fat Bombs

Serves: 6, Preparation Time: 10 minutes, Cooking Time: 15 minutes

Ingredients

- ¼ cup almond flour
- ½ cup dried unsweetened coconut
- 2 tablespoons liquid stevia
- 1 tablespoon vanilla extract
- 1 tablespoon heart-healthy oil
- 3 large egg whites

Instructions

1. Preheat the air fryer at 400⁰F for 5 minutes.
2. Combine all ingredients in a mixing bowl.
3. Form 1 ½ inches balls using your hands.
4. Place in the air fryer basket and cook for 15 minutes at 400⁰F.
5. Serve and enjoy!

Nutrition information:

Calories per serving: 109; Carbohydrates: 5.3 g; Protein: 3.3 g; Fat: 9.3 g; Sugar: 1.1 g; Sodium: 31 mg; Fiber: 1.7 g

Nut-Free Keto Brownie

Serves: 8, Preparation Time: 5 minutes, Cooking Time: 20 minutes

Ingredients

- 6 large eggs
- ½ cup butter, melted
- ¼ cup unsweetened cocoa powder
- ½ teaspoon baking powder
- 2 teaspoons vanilla
- ½ cup cream cheese, softened

- 4 tablespoons liquid stevia
- Cooking spray

Instructions

1. Preheat the air fryer at 350^{0}F for 5 minutes.
2. Combine all ingredients in a mixing bowl.
3. Pour into a greased baking dish.
4. Place in the air fryer basket and cook for 20 minutes at 400^{0}F or if a toothpick inserted in the middle comes out clean.
5. Serve and enjoy!

Nutrition information:

Calories per serving: 220; Carbohydrates: 6.3g; Protein: 6.3 g; Fat: 20.4 g; Sugar: 0.8 g; Sodium: 221 mg; Fiber: 0.2 g

Chocolate Peanut Butter Mug Cake

Serves: 1, Preparation Time: 5 minutes, Cooking Time: 20 minutes

Ingredients

- 2 tablespoons unsweetened cocoa powder
- 2 tablespoon erythritol
- 1 large egg
- 1 tablespoon heavy cream
- ½ teaspoon vanilla extract
- ¼ teaspoon baking powder
- 1 teaspoon butter, softened
- 1 tablespoon peanut butter
- Cooking spray

Instructions

1. Preheat the air fryer at 400^{0}F for 5 minutes.
2. Combine all ingredients in a mixing bowl.
3. Pour into a greased mug.

4. Place in the air fryer basket and cook for 20 minutes at 400⁰F or if a toothpick inserted in the middle comes out clean.
5. Serve and enjoy!

Nutrition information:

Calories per serving: 308; Carbohydrates: 13 g; Protein: 12 g; Fat: 23 g; Sugar: 2.1 g; Sodium: 199 mg; Fiber: 2.9 g

Keto Angel Food Cake

Serves: 8, Preparation Time: 10 minutes, Cooking Time: 30 minutes

Ingredients

- 12 large egg whites
- 2 teaspoons cream of tartar
- A pinch of salt
- 1 cup powdered erythritol
- 1 teaspoon strawberry extract
- ¼ cup butter, melted
- Cooking spray

Instructions

1. Preheat the air fryer for 5 minutes.
2. Mix the egg whites and cream of tartar.
3. Use a hand mixer and whisk until white and fluffy.
4. Add the rest of the ingredients except for the butter and whisk for another minute.
5. Pour into a greased baking dish.
6. Place in the air fryer basket and cook for 30 minutes at 400⁰F or if a toothpick inserted in the middle comes out clean.
7. Drizzle with melted butter once cooled.

Nutrition information:

Calories per serving: 89; Carbohydrates: 6.5 g; Protein: 5.5 g; Fat: 5.9 g; Sugar: 0.5 g; Sodium: 164 mg; Fiber: 0 g

Low Carb Cookie Dough with Sesame Seeds

Serves: 8, Preparation Time: 10 minutes, Cooking Time: 20 minutes

Ingredients

- ¼ cup butter
- 2 tablespoons cream cheese, softened
- 1 large egg
- 1 teaspoon vanilla
- ½ teaspoon stevia powder
- ¾ cup almond flour
- 1/3 cup sesame seeds
- 2 tablespoons unsweetened cocoa powder
- ½ teaspoon coffee espresso powder
- ¼ teaspoon xanthan gum
- Cooking spray

Instructions

1. Preheat the air fryer at 400⁰F for 5 minutes.
2. Combine all ingredients in a mixing bowl.
3. Press into a greased baking dish that will fit in the air fryer.
4. Place in the air fryer basket and cook for 20 minutes at 400⁰F or if a toothpick inserted in the middle comes out clean.
5. Serve and enjoy!

Nutrition information:

Calories per serving: 171; Carbohydrates: 5.3g; Protein: 4.5 g; Fat: 15.5 g; Sugar: 0.7 g; Sodium: 67 mg; Fiber: 2.5 g

Keto Chocolate Banana Brownie

Serves: 12, Preparation Time: 10 minutes, Cooking Time: 30 minutes

Ingredients

- 2 1/3 cups almond flour
- 1/3 cup unsweetened cocoa powder
- 2 1/2 teaspoons baking powder
- ½ teaspoon baking soda
- ½ teaspoon salt
- 1 over-ripe medium banana
- 3 large eggs
- ½ teaspoon stevia powder
- ¼ cup heart-healthy oil
- 1 teaspoon vinegar
- Cooking spray

Instructions

1. Preheat the air fryer at 350^0F for 5 minutes.
2. Combine all ingredients in a food processor and pulse until well combined.
3. Pour into a greased baking dish that will fit in the air fryer.
4. Place in the air fryer basket and cook for 30 minutes at 350^0F or if a toothpick inserted in the middle comes out clean.
5. Serve and enjoy!

Nutrition information:

Calories per serving: 202; Carbohydrates: 8.8 g; Protein: 6.8 g; Fat: 16.8 g; Sugar: 2.2 g; Sodium: 269 mg; Fiber: 3.4 g

Made in the USA
San Bernardino,
CA